Communicative Language Teaching

NEW DIRECTIONS IN LANGUAGE TEACHING

Editors: Howard B. Altman and Peter Strevens

This important new series is for language teachers and others who:
- need to be informed about the key issues facing the language teaching
  profession today;
- want to understanding the theoretical issues underlying current debates;
- wish to relate theory to classroom practice.

In this series:
Communicative Language Teaching: an introduction by William
    Littlewood
*Developing Reading Skills: A practical guide to reading comprehension
    exercises* by Françoise Grellet
Simulations in Language Teaching by Ken Jones

Communicative Language Teaching

An introduction

William Littlewood

Cambridge University Press
Cambridge
London   New York   New Rochelle
Melbourne   Sydney

Published by the Press Syndicate of the University of Cambridge
The Pitt Building, Trumpington Street, Cambridge CB2 1RP
32 East 57th Street, New York, NY 10022, USA
296 Beaconsfield Parade, Middle Park, Melbourne 3206, Australia

First published 1981
Third printing 1983

First printed in the United States of America
Reprinted in Great Britain at the University Press, Cambridge

British Library Cataloguing in Publication Data

Littlewood, William T.

Communicative Language Teaching. – (New directions in language teaching)
1. Language and languages – Study and teaching
I. Title   II. Series
418′.007   P53   80-41563
ISBN 0 521 28154 7

Contents

Acknowledgements

My work at courses and conferences for practising teachers, notably on the British Council London Summer School, has been a stimulus to organise my own ideas on communicative language teaching. I am grateful for all the opportunities for discussion. I am also grateful to Rod Bolitho, Adrian du Plessis, Carl James, Ulla Littlewood and Jerry Moraru, who read and commented on some or all of the chapters. The maps at the end of chapter 4 were designed by David Cobb and are reproduced with his permission.

Introduction

Purpose of the book

The purpose of this book is practical: to help teachers broaden their repertoire of techniques, so that they can enable learners to communicate more effectively in a foreign language.

The book is not intended as a first introduction to foreign language teaching. I have assumed that the reader is already familiar with basic techniques for teaching the structures of a foreign language, such as presenting new language through situations, conducting question-and-answer practice, or using oral drills. My purpose has been to suggest activities through which teachers can help learners to go beyond the mastery of these structures, to the point where they can use them to communicate meanings in real situations.

The discussion is directed mainly towards a teacher whose learners need to acquire a general communicative ability, which will enable them to cope with everyday situations. It is concerned primarily with the type of learner whose needs are described in the Council of Europe's 'Threshold Level', to which I will refer again in chapter 7: 'people who want to prepare themselves, in a general way, to be able to communicate socially on straightforward everyday matters with people from other countries who come their way, and to be able to get around and lead a reasonably normal life when they visit another country'. Accordingly, the main focus of the book is on the development of oral skills rather than the use of the written word, though many of the activities discussed can be adapted to provide practice in writing or reading.

My personal experience of foreign language teaching has been both with adults and with young school learners. In writing this book, I have had both types of learner in mind. It goes without saying, however, that the reader will consider some activities as more suitable for adults, while others are more suitable for schoolchildren. In any case, quite apart from age, groups differ in what they enjoy doing and what helps them to learn most effectively. It is therefore only the individual reader who can judge whether a particular activity is suitable for the groups that he or she teaches.

As I have already indicated, the focus of the book is on the practice rather than on the theory of foreign language teaching. However, if the practice of teaching were completely divorced from theory, it would merely be random activity. I have therefore tried to provide a coherent rationale for the techniques, in the hope that this will help the reader to relate them to the goal of communicative ability and integrate them into his or her own teaching methodology.

Background to the book

The book has its main roots in the so-called 'communicative' movement, which has been influential in foreign language teaching since the early 1970s.

There is nothing new, of course, about the basic idea that communicative ability is the goal of foreign language learning. This is the assumption that underlies such widely used approaches as situational language teaching or the audio-lingual method. If developments since the 1970s have any special claim to the label 'communicative', it is because the implications of this goal have been explored more thoroughly and explicitly than before. These implications form the subject matter of this book, but two of them are so fundamental that I will pick them out in advance:

1 A communicative approach opens up a wider perspective on language. In particular, it makes us consider language not only in terms of its structures (grammar and vocabulary), but also in terms of the communicative functions that it performs. In other words, we begin to look not only at language forms, but also at what people *do* with these forms when they want to communicate with each other. For example, as we shall see in chapter 1, the form 'Why don't you close the door?' might be used for a number of communicative purposes, such as asking a question, making a suggestion or issuing an order.

We can therefore combine the newer *functional* view of language with the traditional *structural* view, in order to achieve a more complete *communicative* perspective. This enables us to give a fuller account of what students have to learn in order to use language as a means of communication. It also suggests an alternative basis for selecting and organising the language items that we need to teach.

2 A communicative approach opens up a wider perspective on language learning. In particular, it makes us more strongly aware that it is not enough to teach learners how to

manipulate the structures of the foreign language. They must also develop strategies for relating these structures to their communicative functions in real situations and real time.

We must therefore provide learners with ample opportunities to use the language themselves for communicative purposes. We must also remember that we are ultimately concerned with developing the learners' ability to take part in the *process of communicating* through language, rather than with their perfect mastery of individual structures (though this may still be a useful step towards the broader goal).

These points will become clearer in the course of the book.

Description of the book

The starting point is a discussion, in chapter 1, of what it means to take a communicative view of language and language learning. The chapter leads to a description of communicative ability, from which I have drawn the main framework for the rest of the book.

The main core of the book (chapters 2 to 6) is concerned with classroom methodology. Chapter 2 discusses some ways in which familiar activities, such as drills, can be adapted so that they help learners to relate language forms more clearly to their communicative functions. Chapter 3, chapter 4 and chapter 5 are all concerned with various kinds of communicative activity, through which learners can increase their ability to convey meanings with the foreign language. Chapter 6 looks at activities for developing learners' listening skills.

Chapter 7 moves the focus from 'how to teach' onto 'what to teach': it considers how a communicative approach might affect the teacher's decisions about the content of a course. Finally, chapter 8 draws some threads together and considers some more general implications of a communicative approach to foreign language teaching.

In a short book such as this, it is obviously impossible to include as much detailed discussion as one would like, either of the underlying rationale or of the practical examples. I have therefore included a section 'Further Reading' at the end of the book. This contains suggestions, chapter by chapter, for readers who would like to pursue the main topics further, whether in a theoretical or in a practical direction. It also identifies publications which I have cited by title only in the text and includes additional references to published teaching materials which exemplify the techniques discussed.

Where I have used specific language-examples, these are in English. Otherwise, however, the activities are equally suitable for learners of other languages. I have taught German and French in addition to English as a foreign language, and have always been aware of the concerns shared by the teachers of different languages, especially where classroom methodology is concerned.

Finally, a word of apology to female readers. The words 'learner' and 'teacher' are conveniently neutral as regards sex, but the English pronoun system has forced me to choose between 'he' and 'she'. The fact that I use 'he' from this point on is of only superficial significance: learners and teachers are female as well as male.

1 What is communicative ability?

1.1 Introduction

One of the most characteristic features of communicative language teaching is that it pays systematic attention to functional as well as structural aspects of language, combining these into a more fully communicative view.

This chapter will look more closely at this communicative view of language, in order to describe the goal of foreign language teaching: communicative ability.

1.2 Structural and functional views of language

The structural view of language concentrates on the grammatical system, describing ways in which linguistic items can be combined. For example, it explains the operations for producing the passive 'The window has been broken' rather than the active 'Somebody has broken the window', and describes the word-order rules that make us interpret 'The girl chased the boy' differently from 'The boy chased the girl'. Intuitive knowledge of these, and of a multitude of other linguistic facts and operations, makes up a native speaker's linguistic competence and enables him to produce new sentences to match the meanings that he needs to express.

The structural view of language has not been in any way superseded by the functional view. However, it is not sufficient on its own to account for how language is used as a means of communication. Let us take as an example a straightforward sentence such as 'Why don't you close the door?'. From a structural viewpoint, it is unambiguously an interrogative. Different grammars may describe it in different terms, but none could argue that its grammatical form is that of a declarative or imperative. From a *functional* viewpoint, however, it is ambiguous. In some circumstances, it may function as a question – for example, the speaker may genuinely wish to know why his companion never closes a certain door. In others, it may function as a command – this would probably be the case if, say, a teacher addressed it to a pupil who had left the classroom door open. In yet other situations, it could be intended (or interpreted, perhaps mistakenly) as a plea, a suggestion, or a complaint. In other words, whereas the sentence's *structure* is stable and straightforward, its *communicative function* is variable and depends on specific situational and social factors.

Just as a single linguistic form can express a number of functions, so also can a single communicative function be expressed by a number of linguistic forms. For example, the speaker who wants somebody to close the door has many linguistic options, including 'Close the door, please', 'Could you please close the door?', 'Would you mind closing the door?', or 'Excuse me, could I trouble you to close the door?'. Some forms might only perform this directive function in the context of certain social relationships – for example, 'You've left the door open!' could serve as a directive from teacher to pupil, but not from teacher to principal. Other forms would depend strongly on shared situational knowledge for their correct interpretation, and could easily be misunderstood (e.g. 'Brrr! It's cold, isn't it?').

1.3 Understanding functional meanings

A teacher wanted a child to pick up a towel and hang it on a rail. His first three attempts to communicate his meaning to the child resulted only in confusion:
'Would you pick up the towel for me, before someone steps on it?' (No action from the child)
'What do we do with the towel, Jimmie?' (Still no action)
'Well, would you like to hang it up?' (No action)
The child only understood when the teacher used a direct imperative:
'Jimmie, pick the towel up!'
It was clear from the child's reactions that he was not being insolent or deliberately uncooperative. This leaves three possible explanations for his failure to understand the teacher's first three attempts to get his meaning across:
– The *structure* of the first three sentences could have been outside the child's linguistic competence. This explanation is unlikely to be valid in this case, but would of course be a strong candidate if the hearer were a foreign learner.
– The child may have been unfamiliar with the use of interrogative structures for expressing commands, perhaps because his parents used predominantly direct imperatives to control his behaviour. In other words, the teacher's first three utterances

v ε

may have been within his *linguistic* competence but outside his *communicative* competence.
- He may not have possessed the appropriate *nonlinguistic* knowledge for understanding the teacher's communicative intention. For example, he needed situational knowledge about where the towel was and where it belonged, as well as social knowledge about the tidiness convention at school (a convention which the teacher's second utterance explicitly appeals to).

These possible explanations highlight three corresponding aspects of the skill involved in understanding meanings:
- the ability to understand linguistic structures and vocabulary;
- knowledge of the *potential* communicative functions of linguistic forms;
- the ability to relate the linguistic forms to appropriate nonlinguistic knowledge, in order to interpret the specific functional meaning intended by the speaker.

An important implication of the third aspect is that the foreign language learner needs more than a 'fixed repertoire' of linguistic forms corresponding to communicative functions. Since the relationship between forms and functions is variable, and cannot be definitely predicted outside specific situations, the learner must also be given opportunities to develop *strategies* for interpreting language in actual use.

negotiated meaning
conveyed meaning
Gumperz?

1.4 Expressing functional meanings

In the preceding section, the incident between teacher and child was presented as showing the hearer's failure to understand. However, communication is a two-sided process, and it could equally well be argued that the speaker had failed to verbalise his message adequately. He had failed to judge the linguistic and nonlinguistic knowledge of the child, and had therefore not selected linguistic forms that would be interpreted as he intended.

conv. inf.

When we speak, we are constantly estimating the hearer's knowledge and assumptions, in order to select language that will be interpreted in accordance with our intended meaning. For example, let us assume that the people in a room know that they have been invited for a meal. The hostess may then utter the single word 'Ready?' as a directive to come to the table and eat. On the other hand, if they do not know that she has been preparing a meal, she must verbalise her meaning in greater detail, for example with 'Would you like to come and have something to eat?'. In each case, she takes account of the knowledge shared between herself and the others, and produces sufficient language to express her communicative purpose in that situation. As with the teacher, of course, she may find that she has overestimated her hearers' knowledge – perhaps the guests to whom she says 'Ready?' do not realise, after all, that they are to have a meal. In this case, again like the teacher, she must use their reaction as feedback about the failure of her attempt, and remedy it with new language.

The most efficient communicator in a foreign language is not always the person who is best at manipulating its structures. It is often the person who is most skilled at processing the complete situation involving himself and his hearer, taking account of what knowledge is already shared between them (e.g. from the situation or from the preceding conversation), and selecting items which will communicate his message effectively. Foreign language learners need opportunities to develop these skills, by being exposed to situations where the emphasis is on using their available resources for communicating meanings as efficiently and economically as possible. Since these resources are limited, this may often entail sacrificing grammatical accuracy in favour of immediate communicative effectiveness.

In the same way as for comprehension, then, the learner needs to acquire not only a repertoire of linguistic items, but also a repertoire of strategies for using them in concrete situations.

1.5 Understanding and expressing social meanings

As we saw in the preceding section, one factor determining the speaker's choice of language is the knowledge that he assumes the hearer to possess. A further important factor is his interpretation of the social situation in which communication is taking place: language carries not only *functional* meaning, it also carries *social* meaning.

The hostess who puts her head round the door and calls 'Ready?' to her guests is not only making assumptions about shared knowledge. She is also signalling her view that the situation is not formal. If she felt otherwise, for example because the guests were business acquaintances rather than personal friends, this would probably cause her to choose different language, such as 'Would you like to come and eat now?'. On an even more formal occasion, the socially appropriate form might be 'Ladies and gentlemen, dinner is served'. Similarly, referring back to the communicative function discussed in an earlier section, a student

levels of formality

might say 'Shut the door, will you?' to a flat-mate, but to a stranger on a train it would be more appropriate to say, for example, 'Excuse me, would you mind closing the door?' To use the formal version with a flat-mate, or the informal version with a stranger, would be equally likely to cause offence.

To a large extent, it is a question of a speaker conforming to linguistic (or rather, *socio*linguistic) conventions in order to be unobtrusive. He may choose socially appropriate speech in so far as his repertoire permits, just as he may choose socially appropriate dress in so far as his wardrobe permits. The process also works the other way, however: as well as the social situation determining the nature of the language, the language can help determine the social atmosphere of the situation. For example, the level of formality of the teacher-pupil relationship can be greatly affected by the level of formality of the teacher's language. In general, the use of informal speech not only reflects but also accelerates the development of a personal relationship. A foreigner may therefore be hindered in forming such relationships if he is unable to adapt his speech to the increasing familiarity and informality of a friendship. In effect, by using 'bookish' grammar, complete sentences and careful pronunciation, he may be sending out signals of formality and social distance unintentionally. Receptively, too, he may be unable to interpret the native speaker's attempts to move towards a more informal basis for the relationship, for example by tentative use of first name and colloquial turns of phrase. Therefore, as learners advance in competence, an important direction of progress is towards greater understanding and mastery of the social significance of alternative language forms. In the earlier stages, however, the emphasis is likely to be on achieving productive mastery of forms from a 'middle' level of formality, which will be acceptable both with friends and with strangers.

Similar considerations apply to other language forms that communicate interpersonal attitudes. Learners are sometimes misled by apparent structural or dictionary equivalents in their own language, which cause them to produce socially offensive forms in the foreign language. For example, Russian learners of English sometimes use the emphatic 'Of course!' in answer to a yes/no question, in a way that seems to suggest that the question is silly and the answer rather obvious. In fact, they are merely transferring a Russian lexical 'equivalent' that has no such overtones; they may remain unaware for years of the unfavourable effect they are producing on English-speaking listeners. Such errors as this are potentially more serious than any other, not least because few native hearers realise that their true source is inadequate learning rather than offensive attitudes.

1.6 Summary

We can now summarise four broad domains of skill which make up a person's communicative competence, and which must be recognised in foreign language teaching. For the sake of simplicity, they are here presented only from the speaker's perspective:
- The learner must attain as high a degree as possible of linguistic competence. That is, he must develop skill in manipulating the linguistic system, to the point where he can use it spontaneously and flexibly in order to express his intended message.
- The learner must distinguish between the forms which he has mastered as part of his linguistic competence, and the communicative functions that they perform. In other words, items mastered as part of a *linguistic* system must also be understood as part of a *communicative* system.
- The learner must develop skills and strategies for using language to communicate meanings as effectively as possible in concrete situations. He must learn to use feedback to judge his success, and if necessary, remedy failure by using different language.
- The learner must become aware of the social meaning of language forms. For many learners, this may not entail the ability to vary their own speech to suit different social circumstances, but rather the ability to use generally acceptable forms and avoid potentially offensive ones.

1.7 Scope of the present book

The first of these four domains is not the main subject-matter of this book. This should not be taken as an attempt to devalue linguistic competence. On the contrary, its importance is here taken for granted: it is one of the undeniable facts about language use that we communicate by exploiting the creative potential of linguistic structures. This has always been recognised in language teaching, and as a result, we possess a wide range of techniques for helping learners to master the linguistic system of a foreign language.

This book will concentrate on ways in which this repertoire of techniques can be adapted and extended, in order to satisfy the broader conception of communicative ability described in this chapter. In particular, it will discuss ways in which:

✓   – Old techniques for controlled practice can be adapted so that the learner is helped to relate language forms to their potential functional and/or social meanings.
     – The learner can be placed in situations where he must use language as an instrument for satisfying immediate communicative needs, and where the criterion for success is functional effectiveness rather than structural accuracy.
     – The learner can be helped to use language as an instrument for social interaction, for example through role-playing activities, in which emphasis is on both the communicative effectiveness and the social acceptability of the language used.

but

2 Relating forms to meanings

2.1 Introduction

The specific techniques discussed in this chapter will already be familiar to many readers. Here, the purpose is to show how they relate the acquisition of linguistic structures and vocabulary to the other three components of communicative ability described in the previous chapter, and how they therefore help to bridge the gap between linguistic and communicative competence.

The learning activities themselves are 'pre-communicative' rather than 'communicative'. That is, they aim to equip the learner with some of the skills required for communication, without actually requiring him to perform communicative acts. The criterion for success is therefore not so much whether he has managed to convey an intended meaning, but rather whether he has produced an acceptable piece of language. However, by emphasising the communicative nature of this language, the activities also aim to help the learner develop links with meaning that will later enable him to use this language for communicative purposes.

The term 'practice', as used here, includes not only activities where the learner's response is expected to be immediate (as in most drills and question-and-answer practice), but also those where the learner has more time to reflect on the operations he is performing (as in most written exercises). Each kind of activity has its role to play in helping learners develop both fluency of behaviour and clarity of understanding in their use of the foreign linguistic system. In each kind of activity, too, the linguistic forms may be more or less strongly related to communicative function and nonlinguistic reality. It is with this relationship that the present chapter is concerned.

This perspective also excludes other important factors which the teacher must control, and which are discussed in other methodological handbooks. One of these is the level of linguistic complexity which the learner is expected to cope with. This must clearly be adjusted to suit his learning stage within the course. Another is the linguistic relationship between prompt and response. At one extreme, the response may be composed largely of material already contained in the prompt, with very little reorganisation (e.g. 'Do you think she's British or American?' – 'She's British'). At the other extreme, the prompt may give little help, since the response is related in meaning rather than in structure (e.g. 'Can you tell me the time, please?' – 'Yes, it's half past eight', or the instruction to 'Describe this scene'). The importance of these factors must not be underestimated. They are crucial in enabling the teacher to adjust the linguistic demands made on learners and gradually extend the linguistic competence on which their communicative ability will ultimately depend. Again, however, the present chapter is concerned with the links that exist between the forms produced and their communicative function.

In the examples, 'P' stands for 'prompt', such as the stimulus in a drill or a question put by the teacher. 'R' is the learner's 'response', whether spoken or written. 'Cues' are devices such as pictures or printed items, which help determine the content of what the learner says.

2.2 Structural practice

This form of practice is included here to provide a point of departure for other, more communicatively oriented activities.

Many of the audio-lingual drills produced up to the end of the 1960s are of this type, where the focus is exclusively on the performance of structural operations. Here, for example, learners must produce the correct form of the simple past:

P: John has written the letter.
R: He wrote it yesterday.
P: John has seen the film.
R: He saw it yesterday. (and so on)

I am not suggesting that learners are never aware of meaning in this sort of activity. However, this awareness is in no way essential to performing the operations, and it is likely that many learners will focus only on the structural changes that they have to make. Indeed, they are encouraged to do this by the nature of the relationship between prompt and response, which belong together only by virtue of their grammatical structure, not because they might be expected to occur together in the course of a real exchange of meanings.

Many teachers now exclude purely structural practice from their repertoire, in favour of the other forms to be discussed in this chapter. Nonetheless, we are still too ignorant about the basic processes of language learning to be able to state dogmatically what can and cannot contribute to them. Structural practice may still be a useful tool, especially when the teacher wishes to focus attention sharply and unambiguously on an important feature of the structural system.

2.3   Relating structure to communicative function

The example just discussed can be easily adapted so that it rehearses the same structural facts, but in language which sounds more communicatively authentic:

P: By the way, has John written that letter yet?
R: Yes, he wrote it yesterday.
P: Has he seen the film yet?
R: Yes, he saw it yesterday.

The items now serve to illustrate communicative facts as well as structural facts: the prompt is an instance not only of a 'perfect interrogative' but also of a question, while the response is not only a 'past declarative' but also a 'reply'. That is, it is now possible to recognise the *communicative function* as well as the *structure* of the linguistic forms. We have begun to take account of the second domain of communicative skill described in chapter 1.

As we also saw in Chapter 1, communicative function is closely bound up with situational context. A further step in providing links between structure and function is therefore to contextualise the language and ask learners to practise responses which would be (a) realistic ways of performing useful communicative acts in (b) situations they might expect to encounter at some time. For example:

Your friend makes a lot of suggestions, but you feel too tired to do anything.
P: Shall we go to the cinema?
R: Oh no, I don't feel like going to the cinema.
P: Shall we have a swim? (*or* What about a swim, then?)
R: Oh no, I don't feel like having a swim.

Structurally, the learner is here practising the use of the gerund. Functionally, he is learning ways of making and rejecting suggestions. This functional aspect can naturally be emphasized by the teacher as he presents the activity. Also, as we shall see in chapter 7, the internal organisation of the course may highlight the communicative functions that students are learning to express, as well as (or even more than) the structures and vocabulary they are learning to use.

In these activities, then, the student is learning to relate language to its communicative function. In the last resort, however, the actual operations are still of a purely structural nature, and may be carried out without conscious attention to meaning or situation. Thus in the activity just discussed, the change from 'Shall we + verb' to 'Oh no, I don't feel like + verb + ing' could be made mechanically even if we substituted a nonsense word for the verb. In other words, though we have begun to take account of the second domain of communicative skill, we have still not entered the third domain. This is where the learners must make linguistic choices that are not mechanical but correspond·to specific meanings to be conveyed.

2.4 Relating language to specific meanings

We take a step in this direction when we make the learner adapt his language so that it reflects some aspect of nonlinguistic reality, such as the concrete situation, a picture, or personal knowledge. For example, in the activity discussed above, the learner may be instructed to respond to the suggestions in accordance with his own likes and dislikes:

P: Shall we go to the cinema?
R: Oh no, I don't feel like going to the cinema.
   or The cinema? Yes, that's a good idea.

Alternatively, he may be given picture cues which indicate which preference he should express:
   (The learner sees a picture of a park)

P: Shall we go to the cinema?
R: No, I'd rather go to the park.

The cue may be provided by the learner's general knowledge:

Contradict or agree with the speaker.
P: Chris Evert-Lloyd plays golf.
R: No she doesn't. She plays tennis.
P: Paris is the capital of Belgium.
R: No it isn't. It's the capital of France.
P: The Rhine flows through Germany.
R: Yes, I know it does.

Question-and-answer activity based on the classroom situation or on visuals, which is so integral a part of 'situational language teaching', requires the learner to relate language to nonlinguistic reality in a similar way. Many teachers now regard these techniques as artificial and lacking any relationship with communicative reality. The teacher asks questions, and the learners make statements about facts which are already known to everybody:

P: Where's the pen?
R: It's on the chair.
P: Where's the chair?
R: It's next to the table.

Such a sequence may therefore be replaced by an activity in which the language is performing a recognisable and useful communicative function, as discussed in the previous section. For example, the learner may be asked to imagine himself giving directions to a stranger, basing his replies on a town plan:

P: Excuse me, where's the post office?
R: It's opposite the theatre.
P: Excuse me, where's the bank?
R: It's next to the cinema.

The realism and relevance of this language offer obvious advantages. In particular, they help to sustain learners' motivation and make the activity more appropriate to their probable communicative needs in the future (a matter which will be discussed further in chapter 7). Nonetheless, since the classroom situation is the nonlinguistic environment which is immediately real to the learners, it remains a convenient aid towards helping them to relate language to external reality.

2.5 Relating language to social context

The activities discussed so far have helped learners to link language forms with (a) communicative functions and (b) specific functional meanings which correspond to aspects of nonlinguistic reality. Students must also learn to relate language to the social meanings that it carries and to use it as a vehicle for social interaction. To this end, it is necessary to increase their sense of performing in a meaningful social context, rather than simply responding to prompts.

An initial step in this direction is to free the activity from dependence on the teacher or tape, so that learners begin to *interact* as equal partners in an exchange, rather than merely *re*acting to stimuli. For example, after an initial period when they learn to make and reject suggestions under the teacher's control (as in preceding sections), they may be asked to interact in pairs. One learner may then have a set of cues indicating what suggestions he has to make, while the other responds either according to personal preference, or from a second set of visual cues.

The stimulus for interaction in pairs may be provided by asking learners to obtain information to complete a questionnaire. For example, it may be a question of discovering each other's preferences between various pairs of items ('S' = 'student'):

(S1 has to complete a questionnaire)

S1: Which do you prefer, tea or coffee?
S2: I prefer tea.
   or I prefer coffee.
   or I like them both.
   or I don't like either.

(And so on, for other items on the questionnaire).

At a later stage, two exchanges may be combined to form a longer conversational sequence. The cues in the following activity might be a list of general and specific alternatives, from which the partners would select their suggestions and preferences:

(The list of alternatives would include:

cinema: detective film, love film
meal: Indian meal, Chinese meal
drink: beer, coffee
concert: jazz concert, classical concert)
S1: Shall we go to the cinema?
S2: No, I'd rather go to a concert.
S1: What kind of concert?
S2: I'd like to hear some jazz.

If the exchange is provided with a beginning and an end, it becomes a coherent dialogue in a recognisable social setting:

(Using the same list of alternatives for cues)

You and your friend have been studying together in the library all afternoon. One of you is now tired of working.
S1: Let's go out now, shall we?
S2: Where to?
S1: How about going for a drink?
S2: Oh – I'd rather have a meal.
S1: What kind of food would you like?
S2: I'd like a Chinese meal.
S1: Good idea. Let's go then.

When learners have acquired adequate command of a suitable repertoire of items, they may use them to perform in an 'open dialogue'. This requires them to identify more strongly with a social role, in order to create whole responses during a piece of social interaction:

You are visiting a friend, Peter.
Peter: Let's have a drink. What would you like, tea or coffee?
You:

Peter: I'll put a record on first. Do you like jazz?
You:
Peter: What do you feel like doing afterwards?
You:
Peter: All right. Well, I'll go and make the tea/coffee.

A similar effect may be achieved through a 'cued dialogue', in which learners interact on the basis of a series of cues. These specify the communicative function to be expressed, but otherwise leave learners to create the interaction themselves, by selecting appropriate language from their repertoire. Learners may have separate role-cards so that, at least the first time the dialogue is performed, there is an element of uncertainty and spontaneity about the interaction:

Partner A	*Partner B*
You meet B in the street.	You meet A in the street.
A: Greet B.	A:
B:	B: Greet A.
A: Ask B where he is going.	A:
B:	B: Say you are going for a walk.
A: Suggest somewhere to go together.	A:
B:	B: Reject A's suggestion. Make a different suggestion.
A: Accept B's suggestion.	A:
B:	B: Express pleasure.

Through these activities the language has become increasingly embedded in a context of social interaction. Gradually, too, the learner's performance has become less controlled by specific linguistic prompts and more controlled by the need to produce language in response to the functional and social demands of social interaction. With open dialogues and cued dialogues, we begin to enter the realm of creative role-playing, which will be discussed in chapter 5.

2.6 Conclusion

This chapter has been concerned primarily with training learners in the 'part-skills' of communication: enabling them to acquire linguistic forms and relate them to communicative function, nonlinguistic reality and social context.

There are no set formulae to determine the teacher's selection from among these activities. His choice can only be determined

14

by his understanding of the ultimate goal and by his judgment of where the learners stand in relation to it. In the early stages of a course, he may expose learners to the same basic linguistic material in sequences of activities similar to the one followed in this chapter, so that they can move gradually towards the ability to participate in meaningful interaction. Later, learners will have achieved greater independence in their learning and use of language. They will therefore be able to move more swiftly from the initial learning of new language to the point where they have integrated it into their repertoire and can use it in more independent forms of interaction.

Open dialogues and cued dialogues already require the learner to develop a moderate degree of independence in using the language he has learned. The next three chapters will discuss activities which provide learners with opportunities to develop further in this direction.

Communicative activities: some general considerations

Introduction

The activities discussed in chapter 2 were described as 'pre-communicative'. By this, I meant that the learner was not engaged in activities where his main purpose was to communicate meanings effectively to a partner. Rather, his main purpose was to produce certain language forms in an acceptable way. He was generally prompted to use these forms by the teacher's instructions (as in a drill). Alternatively, the teacher may have designed the activity so as to provide an opportunity for learners to produce language that they had recently learnt (e.g. through open or cued dialogues). The teacher's overall purpose was to prepare the learner for later communicative activity by providing him with the necessary linguistic forms and the necessary links between forms and meanings. Accordingly, the learner's focus was more on *language forms to be learnt* than on *meanings to be communicated*.

This balance of focus between language forms and meanings is of course a matter of degree, not an all-or-nothing affair. For example, we saw in the case of cued dialogues that the learner had to start from a specific functional meaning and produce acceptable language. In such an activity, it is impossible to state whether an individual learner sees his purpose as being primarily (a) to communicate meanings intelligibly, (b) to produce correct language or (c) to do both in equal proportion. To a large extent, this will depend on how the teacher presents the activity and whether the learner expects his performance to be evaluated according to its communicative effectiveness, its grammatical accuracy, or both. Similarly, in a question-and-answer activity designed to practise a specific structure, the teacher may often make the learners perceive the interaction as more communicative if he responds to the content of what they say as well as to its linguistic form.

We must therefore not think in terms of clear-cut distinctions, but in terms of differences of emphasis. With this important proviso, this chapter and the two that follow will discuss activities that are communicative rather than pre-communicative in nature.

In them, the learner uses the linguistic repertoire he has learnt, in order to communicate specific meanings for specific purposes.

3.2 Purposes of communicative activities

At this stage, it may be useful to consider briefly what the teacher might hope to achieve through communicative activity in the classroom, since this will determine his own attitude towards it and what place he gives it in his overall methodology. I will therefore summarise, under four headings, some of the contributions that communicative activities can make to language learning.

They provide 'whole-task practice'

In considering how people learn to carry out various kinds of skilled performance, it is often useful to distinguish between (a) training in the *part-skills* of which the performance is composed and (b) practice in the *total skill,* sometimes called 'whole-task practice'. Learning to swim, for example, usually involves not only separate practice of individual movements (part-skills), but also actual attempts to swim short distances (whole-task practice). In foreign language learning, our means for providing learners with whole-task practice in the classroom is through various kinds of communicative activity, structured in order to suit the learners' level of ability.

They improve motivation

The learners' ultimate objective is to take part in communication with others. Their motivation to learn is more likely to be sustained if they can see how their classroom learning is related to this objective and helps them to achieve it with increasing success.

Also, most learners' prior conception of language is as a means of communication rather than as a structural system. Their learning is more likely to make sense to them if it can build on this conception rather than contradict it.

They allow natural learning

Language learning takes place inside the learner and, as teachers know to their frequent frustration, many aspects of it are beyond their pedagogical control. It is likely, in fact, that many aspects of language learning can take place only through natural processes, which operate when a person is involved in using the language for communication. If this is so, communicative activity (inside or outside the classroom) is an important part of the total learning process.

They can create a context which supports learning

Communicative activity provides opportunities for positive personal relationships to develop among learners and between learners and teacher. These relationships can help to 'humanise' the classroom and to create an environment that supports the individual in his efforts to learn.

We will return to these last two points in the final chapter of the book.

3.3   Learner-directed activity

In many of the communicative activities which we will be discussing, the teacher creates a situation and sets an activity in motion, but it is the learners themselves who are responsible for conducting the interaction to its conclusion. Often, there will be several groups or pairs performing simultaneously, without the teacher's continuous supervision. For many groups of learners, this responsibility will be unfamiliar at first. Too sudden a transition to undirected activity may therefore create difficulties and tensions which could undermine their confidence, both in themselves and in the teaching methods being used. The teacher needs to bear this factor in mind and be prepared to wean learners gradually from dependence on his own control. For example:
- The teacher can test a group's initial response to undirected activity by introducing it initially in small doses, which he can increase gradually as the learners develop more confidence and independence.
- At first, the teacher must make especially sure that learners understand what they are required to do in an activity. He can demonstrate it himself with members of the class. Also, as we shall see later, some activities can be performed not only in pairs or groups, but also as a class under the teacher's direction.
- The teacher may begin by selecting activities which make comparatively light demands on the learners' linguistic and creative abilities. At several points in the pages which follow, I will point out how the teacher can adjust the difficulty of a

task. Also, we will see a number of activities which can be performed with predetermined language. The teacher can equip the learners specifically with the language forms that they need for these activities, which can serve as a 'bridge' between controlled and uncontrolled language use.

3.4 The teacher's role in communicative activities

Especially in the more creative types of activity, unnecessary intervention on the teacher's part may prevent the learners from becoming genuinely involved in the activity and thus hinder the development of their communicative skills. However, this does not mean that once an activity is in progress, the teacher should become a passive observer. His function becomes less dominant than before, but no less important. For example:

- If learners find themselves unable to cope with the demands of a situation, the teacher can offer advice or provide necessary language items. If pupils cannot agree on any point, he can resolve their disagreement. In other words, he is available as a source of guidance and help. His presence in this capacity may be an important psychological support for many learners, especially for those who are slow to develop independence.
- While learners are performing, the teacher can monitor their strengths and weaknesses. Even though he may not intervene at the time, he can use <u>weaknesses</u> as signs of <u>learning needs</u> which he must cater for later, probably through more controlled, pre-communicative activities, such as those discussed in chapter 2. In this way, he can maintain a constant link between pre-communicative and communicative activities in the course, each type reinforcing and providing input to the other.
- There may be occasions when the teacher decides to exercise a more immediate influence over the language used. Most obviously, he may need to discourage learners from resorting to their mother tongue in moments of difficulty. He may also decide that a particular error is so important that he must correct it at once, to prevent it from becoming fixed in the learners' speech.

In making the above points, I have assumed that the teacher has no direct role in the activity. There will also be activities, of course, in which the teacher can take part as a 'co-communicator'. Provided he can maintain this role without becoming dominant, it enables him to give guidance and stimuli from 'inside' the activity.

19

3.5 Types of communicative activity

In discussing the various examples of communicative activities, I propose to distinguish between two main categories, which I will call 'functional communication activities' and 'social interaction activities'.

Functional communication activities

In chapter 1, we saw that one important aspect of communicative skill is the ability to find language which will convey an intended meaning effectively in a specific situation.

We can devise communicative activities for the classroom which emphasise this *functional* aspect of communication. For example, there may be a problem which learners must solve, or information which they must exchange, *with whatever language they have at their disposal*. That is, they are not required to attempt to choose language which is appropriate to any particular situation. It may not even matter whether the language they use is grammatically accurate. The main purpose of the activity is that learners should use the language they know in order to get meanings across as effectively as possible. Success is measured primarily according to whether they cope with the communicative demands of the immediate situation.

Because of this emphasis on being functionally effective, activities of this type are here called 'functional communication activities'. They will be discussed in chapter 4.

Social interaction activities

We also saw in chapter 1 that another important aspect of communicative skill is the ability to take account of the social meaning as well as the functional meaning of different language forms. The competent speaker chooses language which is not only functionally effective, but is also appropriate to the social situation he is in.

We can devise communication activities which place emphasis on social as well as functional aspects of communication. Learners must still aim to convey meanings effectively, but must also pay greater attention to the social context in which the interaction takes place. Because of the limitations of the classroom, simulation and role-playing are now important techniques for creating a wider variety of social situations and relationships than would otherwise occur.

Success is now measured not only in terms of the functional effectiveness of the language, but also in terms of the acceptability of the forms that are used. In the early stages of learning, acceptability may mean little more than a reasonable degree of accuracy in pronunciation and grammar. Later, it will increasingly come to include producing language which is appropriate to specific kinds of social situation.

Activities of this type are here called 'social interaction activities'. They will be discussed in chapter 5.

As with the initial distinction between pre-communicative and communicative activities, I must now make an important qualification. Once again, we are not dealing with a strict division, but with differences of emphasis. Like 'focus on meanings', attention to the social acceptability of language forms is not an all-or-nothing matter, but a question of varying degree. There is a continuous range of possibilities, including:

- At one extreme, purely functionally oriented activities in which accuracy or appropriacy are irrelevant. The only aim is to exchange meanings successfully in order to complete a task or solve a problem.
- Activities in which learners are required to aim for a minimum degree of social acceptability, perhaps in the form of grammatical accuracy and avoiding causing offence.
- At the other extreme, activities in which learners must aim to produce forms which are fully appropriate to the social context, for example, in level of formality.

The activities discussed in chapter 4 are those which seem to me to belong, by their nature, to the first part of this continuum: the main purpose is always to achieve some practical result. The activities discussed in chapter 5 seem to me to belong more to the later part of the continuum, notably because learners' social roles become more important. However, the individual teacher can generally decide for himself how strongly he wishes to encourage learners to aim for acceptability as well as functional effectiveness in their speech.

3.6 Conclusion

This chapter has discussed some general features of communicative activities. It has also explained the underlying distinction on which the next two chapters are based. We will now turn to considering concrete examples of communicative activities.

4 Functional communication activities

4.1 Introduction

The principle underlying functional communication activities is
that the teacher structures the situation so that learners have to
overcome an information gap or solve a problem. Both the stimulus for communication and the yardstick for success are thus
contained within the situation itself: learners must work towards
a definite solution or decision.

The range of functional communication needs that can be
created for learners is limited by the nature of the classroom situation. It involves mainly the sharing and processing of information. However, through the materials used, there is wide scope
for varying the content and complexity of the language that is
needed.

This chapter will group functional communication activities
according to the two main uses of language just mentioned:
(a) using language to share information and (b) using language to
process information (e.g. to discuss it or evaluate it). Since 'sharing' may or may not be governed by rules which restrict the
learners' freedom to cooperate fully in exchanging information,
we have the following main groups:
1 Sharing information with restricted cooperation.
2 Sharing information with unrestricted cooperation.
3 Sharing and processing information.
4 Processing information.

4.2 Sharing information with restricted cooperation

This type of communicative activity produces the simplest patterns of interaction. The situation is always that one learner (or
group) possesses information which another learner (or group)
must discover. In order to introduce a 'game' element and to
ensure that the interaction lasts long enough to provide sustained
practice, the knower is not allowed to cooperate fully: he provides information only in response to appropriate cues. These are
usually questions of a specified kind (e.g. yes/no questions),

which are capable of eliciting the information gradually but not in one swoop.

Since the learners must in any case interact according to strict rules, it is often possible for the teacher to go as far as specifying the actual language structures that they should use. If he does this, the activity becomes a communicative form of controlled language practice, for which the learners can be specifically equipped with the language they need.

Identifying pictures

Learner A has a set of four, five or six pictures which are all very similar in content, but contain a number of distinguishing features. For example, the pictures below all show a living room, but differ in the colour of the curtains, the number of chairs and the position of the radio:

Learner B has a duplicate copy of just one of these pictures, which he has either been given by the teacher or selected himself from a complete duplicate set. Learner A must find out which of the pictures learner B is holding, by asking him questions about it.

In this activity, the vocabulary that the learners need is determined largely by the subject matter of the pictures. In addition, the teacher can elicit specific structures by manipulating the features that distinguish the individual pictures. For example, in order to distinguish the pictures above, learners would need to ask and answer questions with 'What colour . . . ?', 'How many . . . ?' and 'Where . . . ?'.

The general level of difficulty of the task is determined largely by how numerous, how obvious and how easily describable the distinguishing features are. For example, it would test even a native speaker's communicative ability to describe and distinguish four living rooms if the only distinctive feature were the size of a coffee table. On the other hand, even a beginner could distinguish pictures in which the most important objects were of different colours.

Discovering identical pairs

This activity produces similar kinds of interaction to the one just described, except that the discoverer must now question several other learners.

A similar set of, say, four pictures is now distributed among four learners, who thus have one picture each. A fifth learner in the group holds a duplicate of one of the pictures. He must question the others, in order to discover which learner has the picture identical to his own.

If the teacher wishes, he can present the activity in the guise of a 'detective enquiry'. The discoverer's (i.e. detective's) card shows a picture of a stolen object or wanted person. The learner with the identical card is the thief or criminal's acquaintance.

A further variation, using a slightly different form of organisation, has been entitled 'Find your partner'. The teacher gives one card to each learner in the class or large group (e.g. of 15). Not all the cards are different, however. For example, with a group of 15, there might be five different pictures, with three copies of each. The learners must now circulate and ask each other about their cards, until each has found a partner with a card identical to his own.

'Find your missing friend' is conducted in the same way. The pictures now show people, and there are two copies of each.

One copy indicates that the learner holding it must search for the person shown in the picture. The second copy states that the learner holding it saw the person shown in the picture at a particular time and place. The searcher must find the learner whose picture shows the same person as his own and thus discover when and where his friend was last seen. This activity too can of course be presented in different guises, for example as a detective's search for a wanted criminal.

These pair-seeking activities can also be carried out with information which is presented in linguistic rather than pictorial form. For example, the detective may have to seek somebody whose appearance, background and/or recent actions correspond to the clues printed on his own card. In 'Let's go together', each learner in a class or large group has to select a 'holiday' for himself. He can choose from three possible towns, three possible hotels and three possible months, which the teacher has either printed on cards or written on the blackboard. After making his selection, he must find a learner who has made the same choice, in order to 'go together'.

Discovering sequences or locations

Learner A has a set of, say, six pictures or patterns. These are arranged into a sequence from one to six (either in advance or by A himself). Learner B has the same set of pictures, but these are not in sequence. Learner B must discover the sequence of A's pictures and arrange his own in the same way.

Instead of sequences, learners may have to discover locations. For example, learner A has a map of a town, onto which he places or draws various people or buildings. B has the same map and (if necessary) the same set of pictures showing people or buildings. He has to find out where A has located his pictures, in order to locate his own in identical positions on the map.

Among other possibilities, a plan of a house could be used in place of the map. Again, learner A must place people or objects in various parts of the house, and B must discover where they are in order to place his own in identical positions. It may be a question of discussing not only locations but also actions: thus, a picture of John and a radio in the living room would indicate that 'John is listening to the radio in the living room.' In this way, it is possible to extend the range of language used beyond the simple description of locations.

In activities which involve discovering locations, the map or plan constitutes the learners' initial shared knowledge. As in other communication situations, the degree of communicative difficulty depends in large part on how detailed and informative this shared knowledge is. For example, it is considerably more difficult to describe and discover locations if the map is completely blank, than if a few streets and landmarks are named as reference points. This is one way, then, in which the teacher can adjust the level of task difficulty. Also, as in previous activities, he can vary the ease with which the individual objects and people can be described and distinguished from each other. (This last point only applies, however, if he provides learners with pictures to be placed on the map or plan, rather than asking them to draw the items themselves.)

Discovering missing information

Learner A has information represented in tabular form. For example, he may have a table showing distances between various towns or a football league table showing a summary of each team's results so far (how many games they have played/won/lost/drawn, how many goals they have scored, etc.). However, some items of information have been deleted from the table. Learner B has an identical table, except that different items of information have been deleted. Each learner can therefore complete his own table by asking his partner for the information that he lacks.

As with several previous activities, the teacher may (if he wishes) specify what language forms are to be used. For example, the distances table would require forms such as 'How far is . . . from . . . ?' and 'Which town is . . . miles from . . . ?', while the league table would require forms such as 'How many games have . . . played?' and 'How many goals have . . . scored?'.

Though tables are the most obvious way of presenting information in this type of activity, it can in fact be presented in any other form that makes it clear that some items are missing. For example, each learner might have a map on which the names of some streets and buildings are not marked, or which does not show all of the places visited by a character in a story. By questioning each other, they can obtain the missing information.

It may sometimes be more convenient for only one learner at a time to be involved in obtaining information from the other. For example, learner A might be required to obtain a personal description of a fictitious person, from information possessed by B in verbal or pictorial form, in order to fill in, say, a 'passport application' or a description with blanks.

The questioning can also be structured by means of questionnaires. The learners must ask other members of the class or group for information specified on the duplicated questionnaire, for example about their leisure activities, the town where they come from, or their opinions about current affairs.

Discovering missing features

Learner A has a picture, for example of a street or country scene. Learner B has the same picture, except that various items have been deleted from it. Learner A (i.e. the partner with the *complete* picture) must take the initiative in asking questions. He must find out which details have not been reproduced in B's version of the picture.

A's task involves asking questions based on his own (complete) picture, in order to find out where B's picture is different. The questions themselves will be of a similar kind to those which the teacher might ask in the course of pre-communicative question-and-answer work based on the complete picture. The present activity can therefore provide a convenient communicative follow-up to such teacher-controlled practice, requiring learners to use the same language, but for a different purpose.

Discovering 'secrets'

A large number of communicative activities can be based on the pattern of 'What's my line?' or 'Twenty Questions'. That is: one learner has a piece of 'secret' information, which the others in his class or group must discover by asking appropriate questions.

The questions must be restricted to a certain kind, such as yes/no questions, in order to prevent the discoverers from simply asking directly for the piece of information. Apart from this, in contrast with most of the other activities discussed so far, the lexical and structural content of the language is not predictable: it is up to the questioners to decide what kinds of information will help them to narrow the range of possibilities and discover the 'secret' as quickly as possible. There may be a time limit or, more often, a limit to the number of questions allowed.

The information that the questioners must discover may be of a wide variety of kinds. For example, it may be a profession which the knower pretends to be his own (as in 'What's my line?'); an imaginary identity, such as that of a well-known personality; any concrete object; a country that the knower would like to visit; a secret mission that he supposedly has to carry out; a crime that he has supposedly committed; mundane facts such as where he spent his last holidays; and any number of other possibilities. To some extent, the teacher can adjust the nature of the information with a view to providing a context for certain functions and structures that need to be practised, such as 'talking about past events' or 'talking about intentions'.

The roles of knower and discoverer may be reversed so that the questioner asks about himself rather than about another person. For example, one member of each group may be asked to stand aside, while the others decide on a secret mission for which he has been chosen or a crime of which he has been accused. He must then question the group, in order to discover this information about himself. As a further example, each learner may be allocated a card showing his fictitious identity (or profession, etc.). However, he does not see the card, which is pinned on his back. Each learner has to discover his own identity by questioning somebody else.

Some variations in organisation

The teacher can vary the organisation of these activities to suit specific circumstances.

Each learner has the greatest amount of individual practice when the activity is organised in pairs. It is therefore in that form that most activities have been presented in this chapter. However, a teacher may prefer a different form of organisation if, for example, the class is not yet fully familiar with the activity or the language that it involves; if the class is not yet accustomed to working in pairs; or, of course, if not enough materials are available. Taking as an example the first type of activity discussed above ('identifying pictures'), some alternative forms of organisation are:

- A copy of the complete set of pictures is displayed to the whole class on a poster or by using the overhead projector. One learner selects a picture, either by writing down a number or by taking a picture from a duplicate set reproduced on cards. The other members of the class must question him.
- The class is divided into groups of, say, five or six members each. In turn, each learner selects a picture and is questioned by others in his group. In this way, each individual learner has more opportunities to speak than in (a), but the teacher can still exercise a measure of centralised supervision over the language and behaviour of the class.
- The class is divided into teams. A member of each team in turn selects a picture and is questioned by the other team.

Whatever form of organisation the teacher chooses, he may also introduce an element of competition, by asking learners to carry out the identification task with as few questions as possible.

In this section we have seen a number of activities through which the teacher can create an information gap and thus stimulate simple patterns of communicative interaction. In each case, it is the overcoming of the information gap rather than the production of correct language that signals the success of the performance. In this respect, the focus of the activity is on 'meanings to be communicated' rather than 'linguistic forms to be learnt'. Nonetheless, we have also seen how the linguistic forms that are needed can often be predicted and even specified, so that the teacher may also direct the learners' attention more or less strongly to the forms that they should produce. In this respect, many of the activities in this section provide the teacher with a convenient bridge between pre-communicative and communicative language use: learners are engaged in communicating meanings for a purpose, but they are not yet made to dispense entirely with the 'structural crutches' provided by the teacher. Looking at it from the other direction: learners can be made to practise specific linguistic forms, but move one step further in their ability to use these forms for communicative purposes.

An important price paid for these advantages is that the interaction is still tightly controlled by artificial conventions and consists largely of rigid question-and-answer sequences. This means that a learning group's motivation to perform would inevitably decline if too great a proportion of their time were devoted to such activities. It also means that although we may call them communicative in a technical sense, they still fall well short of the flexible, spontaneous kind of communicative interaction that is the ultimate objective.

4.3   Sharing information with unrestricted cooperation

An initial step towards enabling richer patterns of communication to develop is to reduce the conventions that restrict the cooperation (and therefore the interaction) between learners.

In some of the activities discussed above, a tight framework of rules is a necessary means of sustaining the interaction. In 'discovering secrets', for example, full cooperation would result in the knower simply telling the questioners what they want to know. This is not generally the case, however, when the activity is based on visual information. Here, the information gap is also maintained by the physical fact that the participants cannot see each other's picture (a fact that may be reinforced, if necessary, by setting up a screen). Across this physical gap, the learners' communicative relationship may be allowed to become fully co-operative, with the result that:

- More realistic patterns of interaction can emerge, producing a wider variety of communicative functions. Instead of only asking and answering questions, learners can now use language for describing, suggesting, asking for clarification, helping each other, and so on.
- Faced with the need to cope together with more demanding tasks, learners must develop a wider range of communication skills. For example, they must learn to take shared knowledge into account, to use feedback and reformulate messages when necessary, to compensate for language deficiencies through simplification or paraphrasing, and so on.
- The experience of cooperating through the new language, in order to overcome a mutual obstacle, can help to produce more positive relationships between learners and more positive attitudes towards the foreign language as a means of resolving difficulties.

As I indicated above, many of the activities discussed in the preceding section can be brought into the present category, simply by allowing learners to interact in any way they think fit in order to solve their communication problems. It is for the teacher to decide whether:

- He wishes to sacrifice the control that he was able to exercise over the language used, in favour of the more creative interaction just described. He is likely to do this more often as learners progress. As early as possible in their learning, however, learners need opportunities to be creative with the language they have acquired.
- At a purely practical level, the task may be too easy if learners cooperate, and may not generate enough interaction to justify the organisation involved.

It is not necessary to present for a second time the activities from the previous section that can also be included in the present category. The reader only needs to return to that section, and reconsider the activities as contexts for cooperative rather than restricted interaction. However, there are also a number of more complex tasks that now become possible. This is especially due to the fact that the activities no longer depend on the *discoverer* being able to take the initiative, by formulating relevant questions: it is now possible for the *knower* to take the initiative, by describing what he has in front of him. For example:

30

Communicating patterns and pictures

Learner A has an assortment of shapes which he arranges into a pattern. Learner B has the same shapes. They must communicate with each other so that B can reproduce as exactly as possible the same pattern as A.

Instead of a pattern, the object to be described may be a picture. The teacher may present each learner with a picture to be communicated to a partner, or learners may be asked to draw a picture themselves and then attempt to communicate it. Only in the former case, of course, can the teacher exercise any control over the vocabulary that is needed.

When asking learners to communicate pictures or patterns, the teacher can provide them with initial shared knowledge in the form of identical sheets of card or paper which are marked in some way. For example, the shapes may have to be arranged against a background of numbered squares, to which learners can refer. The pictures may have to be drawn against, say, the out-line of a landscape.

In communicating patterns, the level of difficulty also varies according to how distinct the shapes are from each other. For example, it is considerably easier to describe shapes which differ in easily identifiable ways (e.g. a circle, a square, a triangle, perhaps of different colours) than to distinguish, say, rectangles that differ only in size. The task is still easier if the shapes are recognisable objects, which may be arranged to form a scene.

The two dimensions of difficulty just mentioned (amount of shared knowledge and subtlety of the distinctions to be conveyed) are dimensions of difficulty that exist in all communication situations. By adjusting them, the teacher can therefore equip learners gradually with some of the communicative skills they will need in more complex situations outside the classroom.

Communicating models

This is a variant of the activities just discussed. Learner A (or group A) learns how to construct a model, for example using Lego or some other construction kit. B has the same pieces and must construct an identical model, following A's verbal instructions.

B obviously cannot see A's actions, otherwise he will simply imitate them. However, the teacher may decide to let A see what

B is producing in response to his instructions, so that A has immediate feedback about the success or failure of his communicative efforts.

Similar activities can be based on other operations involving physical action, such as preparing a meal.

Discovering differences

Learner A and learner B each have a picture (or map, pattern etc.). The pictures are identical except for a number of details. For example, two street scenes may be identical except that one of the people is in a different position, one car is a different colour and there is a different number of clouds in the sky. The learners must discuss the pictures in order to discover what the differences are.

A more demanding variant is to distribute a number of pictures among a group of learners. Some pictures are identical, some are different. The learners must first discover how many different pictures there are before, perhaps, also discovering all the distinguishing features.

Following directions

Learner A and learner B have identical maps. Only A knows the exact location of some building or other feature (e.g. a 'hidden treasure'). He must direct B to the correct spot.

In these activities the focus has moved more clearly onto 'meanings to be communicated' for a specific purpose. Because the interaction is more creative and unpredictable, learners will more frequently want to express meanings for which they have not been provided with ready-made linguistic solutions. This means that they will need to develop a wider range of communicative skills and strategies for getting these meanings across. It also means that, in order to communicate effectively, they will sometimes select forms that are not grammatically perfect. The teacher may, of course, use these errors as useful indicators of what still needs to be learnt. However, he should also recognise them as a natural and acceptable phenomenon in any situation where learners have an urgent need to communicate.

4.4 Sharing and processing information

In the activities presented so far, the goal of the communication has been to share factual information. Success has been measured in terms of whether learners gain access to facts possessed by others.

In the activities to be discussed now, a further dimension is added. Learners must not only *share* information, they must also *discuss or evaluate* this information in order to solve a problem. Some consequences are:

- The range of communicative functions that occurs is further widened. In particular, learners will now be involved in going beyond surface facts, in order to analyse, explain and evaluate them.
- This further increases the unpredictability of the interaction. More and more frequently, learners will need to explore their repertoire in order to express ideas for which they have not been specifically prepared.
- There is more scope for disagreement and negotiation. Learners therefore have to manage the interaction more skil- fully at the interpersonal level, for example by learning ways of interrupting or disagreeing without offence.

Many of the activities in this section work on the 'jigsaw' princi- ple: each learner in a pair or group possesses information which is unique to him; he must share it with others; together, the dif- ferent pieces of information provide the material for solving a particular problem.

Reconstructing story-sequences

A picture-strip story (without dialogue) is cut up into its separate pictures. One picture is handed to each member of a group. Without seeing each other's pictures, the learners in the group must decide on the original sequence and reconstruct the story.

There are two levels of language in this activity. The first is the language needed for description and narration. The teacher can exercise some control at this level, through the content of the pictures he selects. The second level is the language needed for discussion. This level is less predictable. However, the teacher can still exercise some control over the general level of difficulty, since this will depend in part on how clearly the pic- tures signal their original sequence. For example, if one of the pictures shows the sun rising and the other shows it overhead, this offers the learners obvious clues to their original sequence. On the other hand, learners may only be able to reconstruct the sequence of some humorous cartoon stories if they understand a subtle point of humour.

The same activity can be performed without pictures. For example, a printed story may be cut up into paragraphs or sections. Each learner within the group (or group within the class) must summarise one section and, perhaps, answer questions put by the others. The whole group or class must then reconstruct the story through discussion. As with the pictures, there are two levels of language involved: the language of the original text (which can be directly controlled by the teacher) and the less predictable language needed for discussion. At the first level, this activity provides a useful context for motivating learners to practise making summaries.

A further variation on this activity is to divide a shorter story into single sentences, to be dealt with in the same way. Learners must now pay closer attention to individual language features which provide clues to the original sequence. With the sentences below, for example, it is necessary to pay careful attention to the use of pronouns and articles, since these exclude every sequence except the one in which the sentences are listed here. Thus not only the level of difficulty of the text, but also the subtlety of the clues, make the sentences suitable for advanced learners:

The magistrates arrived at Colchester's No. 1 court.
They were faced with an embarrassing problem.
A door led from the cells into the dock.
It was jammed and no one could open it.
The police tried and an engineer tried.
Still the lock would not open.
Jim Glossop, 39, was a defendant on a drunk and disorderly charge.
Eventually, he came to the rescue.
He kicked the door open.
The court started its proceedings twenty minutes late.

It should be stressed that in these activities which involve reconstructing story-sequences, each learner can see only one picture, paragraph or sentence. Otherwise, the problem can be solved with only the minimum of verbal communication.

Pooling information to solve a problem

A large number of activities are possible in which learners have to pool information in order to solve a problem. Here, only a few illustrative examples will be presented.
Example (a): Learner A has a train timetable showing the times of trains from X to Y. Learner B has a timetable of trains from Y to Z. For example:

Learner A's information:
Newtown dep. :   11.34   13.31   15.18   16.45
Shrewsbury arr.:   12.22   14.18   16.08   18.25

Learner B's information:
Shrewsbury dep.:   13.02   15.41   16.39   18.46
Swansea arr.   :   17.02   19.19   20.37   22.32

Together, the learners must work out the quickest possible journey from Newtown to Swansea. Again, of course, it is important that they should not be able to *see* each other's information.

Example (b): Learner A has a town plan showing the location of various places of interest. Learner B has a list of opening times and/or a bus timetable. Together, they must devise an itinerary which would enable them to visit, say, five places during one day, spending at least half an hour at each. The places may be specified, or learners may first have to select the ones which would interest them most.

Example (c): An 'army general' at Camp X is in radio contact with another at Camp Y. They must discover a route by which soldiers can travel from X to Y, avoiding natural and enemy obstacles. Each has a map of the terrain which shows some but not all of these obstacles: some obstacles are shown on A's map but not B's, others on B's but not A's, others may be shown on both maps. Through verbal communication alone, the two 'generals' must find a safe route. Depending on how the materials have been constructed, there may be only one possible route, or more than one.

Examples of maps which can be used for this activity are given at the end of this chapter.

The same basic idea can be presented in more everyday terms. For example, it may be a matter of two friends telephoning and discussing the shortest route from one point in the town to another. They must do this by pooling information about one-way streets and roads which are closed to traffic.

Example (d): Each member of a pair or group has information about a different person who is suspected of committing a crime. They must pool this information and analyse it, in order to discover who is guilty. If the clues are not conclusive, they must reach a majority or unanimous decision.

Example (e): Some of these activities can follow on from what has been called 'jigsaw listening'. Each member of the pair or group must first gather his information by listening to a talk or a dialogue. For example, in (d), each learner would first listen to a different conversation, in which a suspect reveals significant facts about himself. The learners would then pool their information in order to solve the problem.

Many of these 'pooling and solving' activities can be organised in two distinct parts. First, learners are asked to pool information in order to complete a table or map. This part of the activity simply involves *sharing* information, in the way described in previous sections (e.g. 'discovering missing information', section 4.2). Then, the learners are asked to solve the problem on the basis of the information that is now before them. Thus, in example (a) above, learners are given not two separate timetables, but incomplete versions of both timetables. The first part of the activity is to share information so that each learner can complete his timetables; the second part is to solve the problem through discussion. This generally makes the overall task less demanding, since it enables the learners to establish a clear basis of shared knowledge before the problem-solving begins.

As I indicated in discussing examples (b) and (c), the teacher can usually choose to structure the materials either so that only one solution is possible, or so that the learners must agree on one of two or more possible solutions.

4.5   Processing information

The last type of functional communication activity dispenses completely with the need to share information. Learners now have access to all the relevant facts. The stimulus for communication comes from the need to discuss and evaluate these facts, in pairs or groups, in order to solve a problem or reach a decision.

The comparative absence of the 'game' element may sometimes result in some slackening of the pressure to communicate. On the other hand, since the problem is now inherent in the facts rather than a result of artificial rules, the activities are more similar to problem-solving situations outside the classroom. Indeed, almost any problem-solving situation from outside the classroom can be used as a basis for discussion. This means that the teacher has considerable scope for adapting the activities to the interests and needs of his pupils.

For example, in an activity included in *Interaction Activities*, learners are asked to imagine that they are going on a three-day camping trip in the mountains. Each person can carry only 25 pounds in weight. Groups must decide what they will take, from the list below, and be prepared to justify their decisions if they are later challenged by other groups.

List

6 lb sleeping bag	3 lb extra pair of shoes
3 lb pack	6 lb water container (full of
1 lb pillow	water)
6 oz small book to record	4 lb camera
what you see	6 lb 3-day supply of food
8 oz swimming suit	12 oz plate, fork, knife, spoon
4 oz soap	12 oz insect repellent
4 oz toothpaste	2 lb extra set of clothing
2 oz toothbrush	3 lb fishing rod
1 lb pot to cook in	6 oz towel
1 lb flashlight	1 oz matches
1 lb rain jacket	

16 ounces = 1 pound; oz = ounce; lb = pound
(1 oz = 28.35g) (1 lb = 0.454 kg)

A similar possibility would be to ask learners to produce an itinerary for a day in London, satisfying the interests of each member of the group. Alternatively, learners could be asked to select gifts for a number of people, taking account of their interests and not exceeding a specified sum of money. Without using prepared materials, the teacher can simply outline a problem-situation and ask groups to choose and justify a course of action. Thus, again in *Interaction Activities,* learners are asked to decide what they would do if they were asked out to dinner and given food that they dislike.

This type of activity may be linked to other, more formal learning activities. For example, when they are working with a reading passage, groups may be given multiple-choice questions to which there are no unambiguously correct answers. They must discuss the possible answers and decide on the most appropriate one. They must also be prepared to justify why they have rejected the others. (*Read and Think* is based on this technique.) As a further example, learners may have to evaluate the social or emotional implications of alternative responses in a dialogue, perhaps also deciding which would be most appropriate in a given context. In addition to these examples, almost any other pedagogical exercise can provide a stimulus for communicative interaction if it is done collaboratively in groups.

Problem-solving activities need not be based only on everyday situations that arise inside or outside the classroom. The teacher may also present more unusual situations, in order to stimulate the learners' ingenuity. For example, he may use a pack of cards in which each card shows a picture of an object or person. Each member of a group must select a card at random from the pack. Together, the group must devise a story which links all the objects or people on the cards. They may later have to satisfy the interrogation of other members of the class about the details of the story. As a further possibility, learners may be required to devise a way of coping with an unusual situation, such as the situation of the thieves in this authentic news item: "Police in London are looking for thieves who shouldn't be difficult to spot, if they still have the stolen goods. Seven cranes, weighing a total of fourteen tons, were taken from a builders' yard last night. . . .'

In these activities, learners must not only analyse information, but also argue, justify and persuade, in order to reach a common decision. They therefore provide a context for a still wider range of communicative functions. They also make it still more necessary for learners to develop skills in managing the interaction at the interpersonal level. In addition, the absence of a single correct answer offers learners scope to express their own individuality through the foreign language. This fact often produces a high degree of personal involvement among the participants.

4.6 Summary

The communicative activities in this chapter follow a general pattern of development. As we progress through the chapter:
- The interaction becomes less controlled by artificial conventions. The activities come to bear greater resemblance to communication situations that learners might encounter outside the classroom.
- The meanings that learners need to express become less predictable. The teacher therefore has less chance of equipping them with the specific language items that they will need. Also, learners must draw on a wider range of skills and strategies in order to get new meanings across.
- There is a gradual increase in the range of communicative functions that is likely to occur. Learners also need to develop greater skills for managing the interaction, e.g. signalling disagreement or interrupting without offence.
- There is increasing opportunity for learners to express their own individuality in discussion.

In other words, learners must gradually become more creative with the language they have acquired. This means that in general, as learners become more competent, the teacher will use a greater proportion of the later activity-types. This is not a firm rule, however. First, as we have seen, the level of difficulty can be adjusted *within* each activity-type. Second, the teacher may sometimes place learners in a situation that makes especially heavy demands on their communicative skills, in order to compel them to explore the full potential of their repertoire and develop strategies to compensate for its weaknesses.

4.7 Some limitations

In this chapter, we have seen how functional communication activities place learners in a situation where they need to use language for a well-defined communicative purpose. They also provide learners with clear feedback about the adequacy of their performance, in the form of the success or failure of their attempts to communicate. In these respects, the activities simulate the demands that will arise outside the classroom, where learners will likewise need to use language to solve immediate communication problems.

However, when we consider further the relationship of functional communication activities to the world outside the classroom, we also see some of their limitations. Three are especially significant:

– The functional meanings which learners have to express are heavily weighted towards sharing and processing factual information. There is a wide range of communicative functions that are unlikely to occur, for example 'greeting', 'inviting', 'asking permission' or 'making offers'.
– The situations in which learners are asked to perform sometimes bear little outward resemblance to those which they will encounter outside the classroom. For example, they are unlikely to have to find matching pictures or sort out jumbled sentences. In this respect, it is significant that some of the activities included in this chapter are often discussed under the label 'communication *games*'.
– Partly as a result of this lack of similarity with real-life situations, the learner's social role is unclear and generally irrelevant to the purely functional purpose of the interaction.

We must therefore extend our range of communicative activities so that learners can (a) experience a wider range of communicative needs in (b) situations more similar to those outside the classroom and (c) under the influence of more varied and clearly defined social conditions. These requirements bring us to the topic of the next chapter: 'social interaction activities'.

Appendix

These maps can be used for the route-finding activity discussed in section 4.4. (Level: advanced. It is possible to devise maps where the task is much easier.)

Learner A's map (learner A is at Camp X)

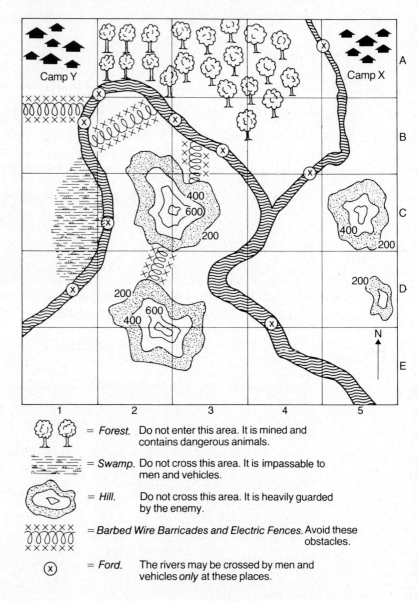

= *Forest.*	Do not enter this area. It is mined and contains dangerous animals.	
= *Swamp.*	Do not cross this area. It is impassable to men and vehicles.	
= *Hill.*	Do not cross this area. It is heavily guarded by the enemy.	
= *Barbed Wire Barricades and Electric Fences.*	Avoid these obstacles.	
= *Ford.*	The rivers may be crossed by men and vehicles *only* at these places.	

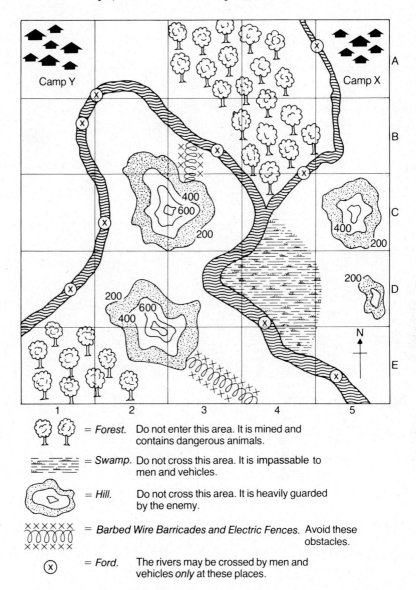

	= Forest.	Do not enter this area. It is mined and contains dangerous animals.
	= Swamp.	Do not cross this area. It is impassable to men and vehicles.
	= Hill.	Do not cross this area. It is heavily guarded by the enemy.
	= Barbed Wire Barricades and Electric Fences.	Avoid these obstacles.
(x)	= Ford.	The rivers may be crossed by men and vehicles *only* at these places.

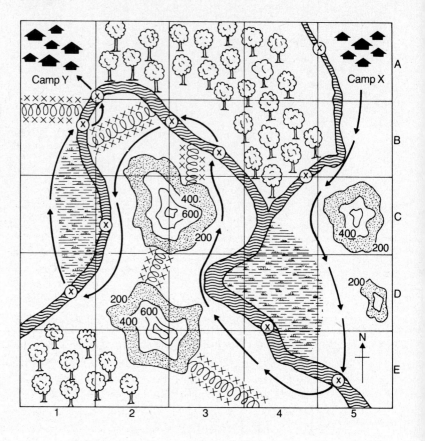

Camp Y

Camp X

400
600
200

400
200

200

200
600
400

N

5 Social interaction activities

5.1 Introduction

Social interaction activities add a further dimension to the functional activities discussed in the previous chapter: that of a more clearly defined social context. This means that learners must pay greater attention to the *social* as well as the *functional* meanings that language conveys. It also means that the activities approximate more closely to the kind of communication situation encountered outside the classroom, where language is not only a functional instrument, but also a form of social behaviour.

In many cases, this further dimension can be added to activities which were discussed in the previous chapter. For example, let us take the communication task in which two friends have to find the shortest route between two points in a town (4.4). This was presented as a purely functional activity, in which learners could solve the problem with any language they had available. It is also possible, however, to ask learners to simulate the *social* roles involved in the interaction. They must then attempt to communicate in ways that are not only functionally effective, but also conform to the social conventions governing how friends would express themselves in that situation. With this extra dimension, the activity then becomes (under the definitions used in this book) a 'social interaction activity', in which:
– The learner is expected to let social as well as functional considerations affect his choice of language.
– Accordingly, the language he produces will be evaluated in terms of its social acceptability as well as its functional effectiveness.
In activities which bear a clear resemblance to recognisable social situations, learners will often not need to be prompted, but will attempt automatically to conform to an appropriate social role in the way they speak. This is not surprising, since they know from their mother tongue that all speech has social as well as functional implications, and that they must aim ultimately for social acceptability as well as functional effectiveness. It is important to remember (as I pointed out in chapter 3) that the distinction between functional communication and social interaction activities is not a strict division but a question of differing

43

emphasis: the precise degree of importance that learners give to social factors during an activity is determined by each individual learner for himself.

Likewise, 'social acceptability' is not a fixed characteristic but a variable quality, depending on what yardstick is being used. For the beginner, it may simply mean achieving a satisfactory level of grammatical accuracy while performing in communicative activities. As the learner progresses, it will come increasingly to mean producing speech which is appropriate (e.g. in level of formality) to the specific situation in which communication is taking place.

This chapter will discuss ways in which the teacher can prepare learners for the varied social contexts in which they will need to perform outside the classroom. First, however, it will briefly consider the classroom itself as a social context for language use.

5.2 The classroom as a social context

The classroom is often called an artificial environment for learning and using a foreign language. If we take as our yardstick for what is 'real' the situations outside the classroom for which learners are being prepared, this is undoubtedly the case. However, we should not forget that the classroom is also a real social context in its own right, where learners and teacher enter into equally real social relationships with each other. It is true that language teaching aims to equip learners for different contexts and that they will later have no cause to, say, 'ask where the chalk is' or 'explain why their homework is late'. However, they will still have cause to 'ask about locations' or 'offer explanations', based on similar forms of language and perhaps differing only in individual vocabulary items.

In other words, the usefulness of language learning does not depend only on what specific pieces of language the learner encounters. Still more, it depends on whether he masters the more general principles which underlie them. Language structures and communicative functions are not bound to specific situations: once they have been mastered so that they can be used creatively, they can be transferred to contexts other than the one where they were initially acquired. That is why, in our mother tongue, we can acquire the basic communication skills in the close family context, and transfer them in later life to a much wider range of social situations. In the same way, the structures and skills that a foreign language learner acquires during classroom interaction can later be transferred to other kinds of situation. This is particularly important for young school learners, who do not yet have a clear perception of the situations in which they will eventually need the foreign language.

In the pages that follow, I will look briefly at four approaches to exploiting the classroom environment as a social context for foreign language use, namely:

1 Using the foreign language for classroom management.
2 Using the foreign language as a teaching medium.
3 Conversation or discussion sessions.
4 Basing dialogues and role-plays on school experience.

The second and fourth of these approaches are applicable to school-age learners rather than to adults.

Using the foreign language for classroom management

This approach involves exploiting for language learning not only the planned activities, but also the classroom management that revolves around them. The lesson has to be begun and ended, individual activities have to be organised, practical problems arise, and so on. This provides a rich source of communicative needs in the foreign language classroom.

Many teachers use the learners' mother tongue in this aspect of their work. This may often be a necessary decision, in the interests of organising the lessons clearly and efficiently. However, it also means sacrificing valuable opportunities for well-motivated foreign language use. In addition, it tends to devalue the foreign language as a vehicle for communication: learners see it as allocated to communicatively non-essential domains such as drills or dialogue practice, while the mother tongue remains the appropriate medium for discussing matters of immediate importance. Many learners are likely to remain unconvinced by our attempts to make them accept the foreign language as an effective means of satisfying their communicative needs, if we abandon it ourselves as soon as such needs arise in the immediate classroom situation.

It is therefore important to provide learners as soon as possible with the language needed for routine classroom affairs, in order to establish the foreign language as the medium for organising learning activities.

Using the foreign language as a teaching medium

For the young school learner, it is generally true that foreign language lessons are more concerned than any other with the

45

development of communicative ability. It is therefore ironical that their syllabus contains the least amount of concrete, nonlinguistic subject matter which might give them the *motivation* to communicate. One approach to this dilemma is to introduce into language lessons the element that they lack: nonlinguistic subject matter which must be learnt and explored through the foreign language.

The actual balance between learning a language and learning *through* a language is infinitely variable:

- At one extreme, there are bilingual schools in which all or most of the lessons are conducted in a non-native language. In Canadian 'immersion classes', for example, English-speaking children begin their education by learning all subjects through French. According to reports, they reach a high degree of proficiency in the second language without receiving formal instruction in it, and do not suffer in other aspects of their education.
- The same principle has led some schools to establish a bilingual section in a modified form. Learners have a small number of formal language lessons. In addition, they study one or two of their other school subjects (e.g. history and/or geography) through the medium of the foreign language. Again, reports suggest that they gain a higher level of proficiency than would otherwise have been the case.
- At the other extreme, an individual language teacher may decide to devote a small proportion of class time (e.g. one lesson per week) to teaching another subject through the foreign language. This may be directly related to the foreign country, e.g. its history, geography, literature or cultural background. The teaching then has a dual role: to provide learners with useful knowledge, and to engage them in purposeful communication in the foreign language.

For the majority of individual teachers, only the third possibility is feasible. Nonetheless, the success of the first two approaches should serve to reinforce the general view that communicative skills develop well in situations where the foreign language is experienced not merely for its own sake, but also as a means towards some other, nonlinguistic end.

Conversation or discussion sessions

The conversation session is sometimes regarded as a source of relief from more 'serious' language work. This should not prevent us from recognising the important functions it can perform in helping to develop communicative ability. For example:

- It opens up a rich stimulus for communicative interaction, namely the varied experiences, interests and opinions of the learners. These may be complemented by written or visual materials which bring further aspects of the outside world into the classroom.
- It thus provides a context for a wide range of communicative functions and domains of meaning. In addition, learners must practise the skills required for managing longer sessions of social interaction, such as introducing a new topic, turn-taking or sustaining the conversation through difficult periods.
- It provides learners with opportunities to express their own personality and experience through the foreign language. It also gives them valuable experience in using the language as a means of handling their own social relationships.

Teachers sometimes allow the teacher-learner relationship to dominate the conversation session so strongly that it produces a typical pedagogical form of interaction: the teacher always initiates, the learner only responds. This greatly limits the communicative functions that learners need to use and the interactional skills they need to practise. If the conversation session is to perform its proper role as social interaction activity, the teacher must perform as 'co-communicator' rather than 'director'. He may guide and stimulate, but not take away the learners' responsibility as equal participants in the interaction. He must also restrain any urge to intervene at every hesitation or false start. These are inevitable when learners are seeking ways of expressing meanings which they may never before have encountered in the foreign language.

The dangers of excessive teacher domination may often be reduced by introducing more informal seating arrangements. When the teacher faces the whole class, his position reinforces his authority as 'knower'. A more informal layout, for example in a circle, can help greatly to reinforce the learners' equality as co-communicators. The teacher may also decide to divide a class into independent groups, as in the problem-solving activities of the previous chapter (4.5). He must then provide materials or instructions that are capable of sustaining the interaction without his presence. For example, he may require each group to formulate its opinions on a number of concrete points, before reporting back to the whole class for a period of 'plenary' discussion.

Basing dialogues and role-plays on school experience

The main supporters of this approach see it as performing a 'therapeutic' as well as a linguistic function. Through foreign language activities, the aim is to help young learners to understand their environment and cope with its problems. To this end, aspects of their experience (such as homework, worry about low marks, conflict with adults) are discussed in class through the foreign language. They are also made the theme of dialogues and role-playing activities. For example, after a discussion about why children fail at school, the teacher and/or learners might compose a dialogue like the following (alternatively, the dialogue might be presented first, and serve as a springboard for subsequent discussion and role-playing):

Edith: Where's Elizabeth these days? I haven't seen her for ages.
Molly: Elizabeth? She's left school.
Edith: Not intelligent enough, eh?
Molly: Rubbish! She's as intelligent as you and me.
Edith: It serves her right. She never did her homework, did she? I always do mine.
Molly: You needn't boast. Your mother keeps you at it. And your father helps you with maths.
Edith: What's that got to do with it?

The teacher can vary the sequence as he thinks fit. Sometimes, discussion may lead to role-playing and then to dialogues composed by learners; at other times, set dialogues may stimulate discussion which leads to role-plays and the composing of related dialogues; and so on.

This fourth approach integrates several features from the preceding ones, for example:

- It exploits for foreign language learning the communicative needs stimulated by the environment in which learning takes place.
- In exploring the problems of the learners' world, it introduces into the language classroom a nonlinguistic subject matter which motivates communication.
- It uses discussion as an important means for simultaneously exploring this subject matter and developing learners' communicative competence.

In its use of dialogues and role-playing, it also leads us into the field of simulation, with which this chapter will now be primarily concerned.

Some limitations of the classroom situation

We have now considered some of the possibilities for social interaction that lie within the classroom situation. However, we must also recognise some of its limitations. In particular:

– In situations outside the classroom, learners will need to satisfy a much wider variety of communicative needs, arising from the events of everyday life.
– They will need to cope with a greater variety of patterns of interaction. These may vary from the formal interview, with its   X tightly controlled structure, to the informal gathering, where everybody competes on an equal basis for turns to speak.
– They will need to become involved in different kinds of social relationship, for which different kinds of language will be appropriate.   *formality*

In order to prepare learners to cope with these wider functional and social needs, we must look for ways of extending the possibilities for communicative interaction in the classroom.

5.3   Simulation and role-playing

In looking for ways of creating more varied forms of interaction in the classroom, teachers of foreign languages (like their colleagues in mother-tongue teaching) have turned increasingly to the field of simulation and, within that field, especially role-playing. With these techniques:
– Learners are asked to imagine themselves in a situation which could occur outside the classroom. This could be anything from a simple occurrence like meeting a friend in the street, to a much more complex event such as a series of business negotiations.
– They are asked to adopt a specific role in this situation. In some cases, they may simply have to act as themselves. In others, they may have to adopt a simulated identity.
– They are asked to behave as if the situation really existed, in accordance with their roles.

In the form that I have just presented them, these same requirements are present during many pre-communicative activities. In chapter 2, for example, we saw activities where learners must project themselves into an imaginary situation, in order to 'make suggestions', 'express preferences' and so on. At an even more superficial level, the same processes occur when learners are asked to perform dialogues which they have memorised. In other words, simulation and role-playing are well-established as techniques for organising controlled, pre-communicative language practice. In this chapter, we have to consider how these techniques can be extended into the field of communicative activities, where:

49

- The learners' focus should be more firmly on the communication of meanings, rather than on the practice of language.
- Learners must identify with their roles in the interaction more deeply than during controlled language practice. If they do not, they will not be able to identify with the meanings being communicated through these roles.
- Learners must create the interaction themselves, on the basis of their roles and the meanings that arise, rather than perform in ways that have been predetermined by the teacher.

We are again dealing here with matters of degree, of course, not with clear-cut distinctions. In any case, the extent to which learners identify with the roles and meanings depends ultimately not on the teacher, but on the individual learner. However, the teacher can adjust the nature of his own control over the activity, in order to allow greater or lesser scope for the learners' creative involvement in it.

In the discussion that follows, the nature of the control exercised by the teacher (mostly through the materials that he uses) is the main criterion for grouping the examples of role-playing activities. As this control becomes less tight and specific, so there is increased scope for the learners' creativity. In this respect, the activities can be viewed as part of a single continuum which links pre-communicative and communicative activities:

Control   ↑   Performing memorised dialogues

            │   Contextualised drills

            │   Cued dialogues

            │   Role-playing

Creativity ↓   Improvisation

All of these activities involve simulation, but differ in terms of teacher-control and learner-creativity. Thus in dialogue-performance, the teacher's control is at a maximum and the learner's creativity is at a minimum. In contextualised drills (e.g. of the kind discussed in chapter 2), the learner creates sentences that may be new to him, but they have been predetermined by the teacher. In cued dialogues, we are on the borderline between pre-communicative and communicative simulation: the teacher exercises direct control over the meanings that are expressed, but not over the language that is used for expressing them (though he may exercise *indirect* control, by previously equipping the learners with suitable forms). In the more creative types of role-playing, as we shall see, the teacher controls only the situation and the learners' roles in it, but leaves the learners themselves to create the interaction.

Along this continuum, I propose to take *cued dialogues* as the point where role-playing becomes sufficiently creative for us to think in terms of communicative language use. There is thus an overlap with chapter 2, where cued dialogues were included among pre-communicative forms of practice. This overlap is intentional, in order to emphasise the continuity that exists between the different techniques.

Role-playing controlled through cued dialogues

The example used in chapter 2 can be repeated here:

Learner A	Learner B
You meet B in the street.	You meet A in the street.
A: Greet B.	A:
B:	B: Greet A.
A: Ask B where he is going.	A:
B:	B: Say you are going for a walk.
A: Suggest somewhere to go together.	A:
B:	B: Reject A's suggestion. Make a different suggestion.
A: Accept B's suggestion.	A:
B:	B: Express pleasure.

Now that we are considering the potential of cued dialogues as simple role-playing activities rather than as controlled language practice, a few additional observations are necessary.

Learners will normally have their cues printed on separate cards. This gives the interaction some of the uncertainty and spontaneity involved in 'real' communication: each learner must listen to his partner before formulating a definite response. On the other hand, the cues enable them to predict a large proportion of what the other will say and, of course, to prepare the general gist of their own responses. This makes it easier for a learner to draw on language forms that he would have difficulty in using with complete spontaneity. The teacher can therefore use cued dialogues to elicit forms which he has just taught or which his learners would otherwise avoid. This use of the forms in a 'semi-communicative' context helps to prepare learners to use them later in fully spontaneous interaction.

previously to the leader of a local pop group. It does about twenty miles to the gallon. Your firm offers a three-month guarantee and can arrange hire purchase. The price you are asking for the car is £1,400.

During the activity, the learners' attention might be focused on a picture of the car in question, in order to add realism and avoid misunderstandings about its appearance.

In this role-play, learners are initially aware only of the overall situation and their own goals in it. They must negotiate the interaction itself as it unfolds, each partner responding spontaneously to the other's communicative acts and strategies.

As a further example on a somewhat larger scale, we might take the published role-playing activity *Detective*. This involves up to six participants: five 'suspects' and one 'detective'. Each suspect has (a) an identical plan of a house where a murder was committed, showing where and when the body was found; (b) information relating to his own role: his identity, attitudes towards the dead man and the other suspects, movements on the previous evening, and so on. One suspect's card states that the holder is, in fact, the guilty person.

The detective has similar information about the circumstances of the crime. When the suspects are assembled, he has to interrogate them and eventually arrest the one he believes to be guilty. Although his instructions are in the form of cues, they are at such a general level that the actual course of the interaction is unpredictable.

Ask them about their names and identity.
Ask them about their movements from 9.00 to 9.30 last night.
Ask them for their ideas about the murderer.
Arrest the murderer.

Once the activity is in progress, it is the detective who exercises general control over the interaction, by virtue of his role and the authority it gives him. This 'internal control' is a convenient way of ensuring that the interaction follows a reasonably ordered course – that everybody speaks, that the proceedings are terminated (through the 'arrest'), and so on. It becomes especially necessary as the teacher reduces his own direct control over the activity and as the participants become more numerous.

The learners' increased responsibility also makes it more important to ensure that they have adequate shared knowledge about matters essential to the interaction. Otherwise, they may form conflicting assumptions which make them talk at cross-purposes. For example, in the car-showroom activity, learners could easily reach an impasse if one assumed the car to be small and modern, while the other assumed it to be large and old. It is only through intuition and experience that the teacher can decide about (a) knowledge which all learners must share if the interaction is to succeed; (b) aspects of the situation and roles which can be left to each individual's imagination; and (c) facts that should be known to one or two learners, but not all. As in every other kind of spontaneous interaction, it is this balance between 'shared knowledge' and 'uncertainty' that provides the necessary impetus for communication.

Role-playing in the form of debate or discussion

This is a variation of the kind of role-playing activity just discussed. The situation is a debate or discussion about a real or simulated issue. The learners' roles ensure that they have (a) adequate shared knowledge about the issue and (b) different opinions or interests to defend. At the end of the activity, they may have to reach a concrete decision or put the issue to a vote. For example, here is an activity from *Over to you*. Learners work in groups of four.

You are a group of people who are anxious to help the old in your small town, and you have managed to make a start by collecting £1,000 from local inhabitants and holding jumble sales.
Study your role and then discuss how the money can best be used.

Student A: Role: Miss Julia Jenkins, spinster.
You feel that you should contact one of the charity organisations advertised on pages 94–95 [of *Over to you*], at least for advice.

Student B: Role: Rev. Ronald Rix, the local vicar.
You wish to found an Old People's Club which will meet in the church hall. Some of the £1,000 that has been collected was raised by holding jumble sales in the church hall.

Student C: Role: Mr David Hicks, headmaster of the local primary school.
You are anxious for the pupils at your school to play a role in helping the aged.

Student D: Role: Mrs Dorothy Foster, widow.
You think the money should be used to renovate an old country house which could be used as an old people's recreation centre.

The skills that learners need to practise are similar to those in the problem-solving activities presented in the last part of chapter 4 (4.5), except that here the social constraints are stronger. The activity is also similar in nature to the discussion sessions mentioned in the first part of the present chapter (5.2). Here, the simulated roles ensure that there will be sufficient conflict of opinion to sustain the interaction.

An example on a larger scale is the published role-play *Pop Festival*. There are three components:

- All learners must assimilate background information, in written and pictorial form, about a quiet country village and a proposal to site a pop festival near it.
- The class is divided into eight groups with conflicting interests: pop fans, festival organisers, farmers, village residents, a local family, the district council and the Department of the Environment. Each group must decide where its own interests lie and formulate its policy. The role-cards pinpoint some of the proposal's advantages and disadvantages.
- A 'public meeting' takes place, involving all groups together. The proposal is debated and a vote may be taken.

This example illustrates how a role-playing activity may integrate a number of different kinds of language activity, involving a variety of skills. Thus:

- Learners must first digest the information relevant to the issue. This involves them in reading. In other activities, it might also involve them in listening to talks or discussions. More advanced learners may be required to gather information through independent enquiry.
- In the second part, learners must discuss in a small-group context, where the rules for speaking are informal.
- They must present their views in a more public context. Here, there are stricter rules governing who speaks when and to whom, and a higher level of formality is expected.
- If he wished, the teacher could add one or more further components. For example, after the public meeting, each separate group could be asked to reassemble in order to compile a written report or newspaper article.

Large-scale simulation activities

We have seen from the discussion of *Pop Festival* how a role-playing activity can consist of a number of interrelated components. The logical extension of this is the large-scale simulation exercise, which may be as long and as complex as time and resources permit. For example, *North Sea Challenge* consists of three 'modules', each expected to last three or four hours:

- In module 1, each group of four or five learners represents an oil company which has just made a successful strike. After studying the relevant background information, they must evaluate the different possible ways of developing the field, and reach a decision on the best way.

– In module 2, the learners are oil-pollution officers. They have to decide how to deal with a major spillage problem.
– Module 3 is similar in format to *Pop Festival*. There is a proposal to site a steel platform construction yard near one of two small Scottish communities. Learners are assigned to groups with different attitudes and interests. Each group must prepare its case for or against the development, then debate the issue at a public meeting.

In some extended simulation exercises, gaming conventions are used in order to simulate the rewards and sanctions that motivate real-life interaction. For example, in *North Sea Exploration,* groups of learners form 'companies' drilling for gas and oil. Each learner has detailed information relevant to his own role in the company (engineer, surveyor, etc.). Each company must discuss and decide where to drill, and what equipment to hire. Chance now becomes important. Every company selects a 'weather card' which determines whether drilling can take place; 'news bulletins' introduce other unpredictable factors; and a 'master resource list' tells the companies the value of their strikes (if any). After each 'round', the companies hold separate meetings again, in order to review their results and formulate their plans for the next round. After a specified time or number of rounds, an overall winner is declared.

Large-scale simulation exercises have been most commonly used outside foreign language teaching, for example in geography (for which *North Sea Exploration* was devised) or decision-making (*North Sea Challenge*). They have similar potential for advanced foreign language work, since they provide just what these learners require: a realistic and integrated context for foreign language use. It is for this reason that *North Sea Challenge* is published both as a decision-making exercise for British secondary schools, and as the 'language use' component in a language-training pack for foreign learners of English. *Pop Festival,* too, is used to develop communication skills in both native speakers and foreign learners of English.

This common ground between foreign language teaching and other educational domains has one important practical consequence for the foreign language teacher: he is increasingly likely to find stimulating ideas and suitable materials by keeping his eye on developments outside his own specialist field.

Improvisation

Improvisation, too, is closely associated with work in the native-language context, notably in drama. It is the last type of role-playing activity to be discussed in this chapter, and the least controlled. Learners are often presented only with a stimulus-situation, which they can interpret and exploit in any way they wish. They may also be asked to adopt particular identities or personality-types, but not necessarily to pursue any particular communicative purposes.

The starting point for an improvisation may be a simple everyday situation into which the learners are asked to project themselves. For example, they could be asked to improvise (in pairs) a scene in which a visitor to their town asks advice about what is worth seeing, or (in pairs or groups) a meeting between old friends who have not seen each other for several years.

In other cases, the situation may be less ordinary and demand more imagination and dramatic effort (which can be a strong motivating force for some groups). For example, groups of six may be asked to act out the stages in this scene, in which tension grows and is finally resolved (the teacher can indicate when the stages begin and end).

You are travelling on an underground train (a subway). Suddenly it stops between two stations. At first you take no notice, but soon you all begin to wonder what is happening. It gets warmer and warmer. You become more and more nervous. After ten minutes, to your relief, the train begins to move again.

For some activities, there may be more emphasis on identifying with certain types of character. For example, working in pairs or groups, learners may be told to imagine that they are the people shown in a particular photograph. They have to decide what events have led up to the situation shown in the photo and improvise what happens next. A similar type of activity can take place if learners are given the first few lines of a dialogue and told to continue it.

In some improvisation activities (such as the train example above), the teacher may decide that the richest interaction is likely to occur if he simply outlines the situation and lets the learners perform impromptu. In others, such as the improvisation based on photographs, he may first ask learners to agree on an interpretation of the situation and their attitudes to each other, so that they have a firmer basis of shared assumptions. In many cases, of course, this preparation may provide a context which stimulates as much creative language use between learners as the improvisation itself.

An alternative form that preparatory work may take is that the teacher first assembles groups of learners who will be performing the *same* role in the planned improvisation. Each group can then discuss the implications and possibilities of one particular role. The learners must then reassemble into groups consisting of learners with *different* roles, so that the improvisation itself can take place. As an example of this procedure, we might take an activity from *Feelings.* The stimulus–situation is presented as follows:

Second thoughts

HAD ENOUGH OF THE RAT-RACE? Would you like to join a small community who are trying to find a less competitive and more peaceful way of life? We have bought a large old farm on the island of Skerry in the Hebrides, and need like-minded people with any practical skills who can make a real contribution to the community. No electricity. Lots of hard work. We aim to be self-sufficient. Box no. 412.

Three years after this advertisement appeared in *The Times,* a television crew visited Skerry to find out how well the community was surviving. They found that many of the people there were very disillusioned, and were thinking of leaving.

The learners are first asked to work in five groups where each member has the same role, in order to work out what to say at the interview.

Group A: You are a reporter. You interview four people to find out how they feel about life in the community.

Group B: You are Jim, a carpenter with a wife and two children.

Group C: You are Shirley. You went to the island after having got a degree in agriculture.

Group D: You are Gerald. You gave up your job as a primary school teacher to go and live in the community.

Group E: You are Miranda, a former art student. You and your husband were working in agriculture before you joined the community.

After this discussion phase, the learners are asked to form new groups and improvise the interview.

The initial preparation in homogeneous groups could, of course, precede many of the role-playing activities discussed in earlier sections. It seems especially appropriate in the present context because the instructions for each role allow such wide scope for individual interpretation. It is, in fact, above all this lack of specific detail about each person's opinions or attitudes that distinguishes the example above from, say, the activity from *Over to you* which I discussed earlier.

There is thus no distinct borderline between what I here

categorise as 'improvisation', and the other forms of role-play
discussed in this chapter. Improvisation is simply one end of the
'control-creativity' continuum on which the whole discussion
of role-playing has been based. It is the form of role-playing in
which learners can be most creative, because they are most able
to act out personal interpretations of the situation and their roles
in it. Indeed, they have even more freedom than in situations
outside the classroom, where they have to obey stronger external
constraints on what they say and do. In this respect, improvisation is not a way of preparing learners to cope with specific
communicative needs. Rather, it is a way of encouraging general
confidence and fluency in foreign language use, by allowing the
learners to explore and exploit their communicative repertoire in
any ways they wish. It also encourages them to express their
own imagination and individuality through the foreign language.
This in turn helps them to relate the new language to their own
personality and to increase their sense of emotional security in
handling the foreign medium.

Finally, a point which applies not only to improvisation, but
to any kind of role-playing activity that does not extend over too
long a period of time. The learners obviously enjoy the greatest
amount of foreign language practice when all pairs or groups
perform at the same time. Nonetheless, the teacher may sometimes feel that they will be stimulated by seeing – and perhaps
discussing – each other's work. This does not necessarily mean
that groups must perform in turn before the whole class, which
can often prove both time-consuming and daunting. It may also
be that, after groups have worked separately, each group links
up with just one or two other groups, so that they can observe
and comment on each other's work. Whatever procedure is used,
the effect of outside observers on the speakers may be similar to
the effect of social norms: they encourage the learners to aim not
only for functional effectiveness, but also for the highest possible
degree of acceptability in their speech.

5.4 Social interaction activities: concluding remarks

In this chapter, we have seen a number of techniques through
which the teacher can create opportunities for social interaction
in the foreign language classroom. Some of these techniques
accept the reality of the classroom situation itself. Others use
simulation as a means of overcoming, to some extent at least,
the limitations of the classroom.

In considering what kinds of activity, situation and role are

best suited to a specific learning group, the teacher must consider
a number of factors, including the following:

- It goes without saying that he must match the linguistic
  demands of an activity as closely as possible with the linguistic
  capabilities of his learners. The idea of 'capability' here covers
  not only the level of complexity of the language forms that
  learners can handle, but also the degree of independence with
  which they can handle them. Thus, as learners increase their
  linguistic competence, there will be scope for both greater
  complexity and greater independence.
- The teacher should remember the point made in connection
  with classroom interaction, that structures and functions are
  not bound to specific situations. Therefore, the situations that
  he selects do not have to be restricted to those in which
  learners expect to perform outside the classroom. Communication skills can be developed in the context of, say, a
  classroom discussion or a simulated detective enquiry, and
  later be transferred to other contexts of language use.
- On the other hand, the teacher has to aim for maximum
  efficiency and economy in his students' learning. It therefore
  makes sense to engage them in a large proportion of situations
  which bear as direct a resemblance as possible to the situations
  where they will later need to use their communicative skills. In
  this way, he can be confident that most aspects of the language
  practised (functions, structures, vocabulary and interpersonal
  skills) are relevant to learners' needs. This is particularly important with older learners, whose needs are comparatively
  well-defined.
- The situations must be capable of stimulating learners to a
  high degree of communicative involvement. In part, this is
  another aspect of the point just made: learners are more likely
  to feel involved in situations where they can see the relevance
  of what they are doing and learning. In part, however, it is a
  separate point. Many learners (notably younger learners)
  have no clear conception of their future needs with the foreign
  language. They may therefore find greater stimulation in
  situations that are of *immediate* rather than future relevance.
  These may be situations which arise in the course of classroom
  interaction. If simulation is used, they may be role-playing
  activities based on their familiar realms of experience (e.g.,
  family, friends or school), rather than those which project
  into a less familiar future (e.g., booking hotels).
- Similar considerations apply to the roles that learners are asked
  to perform in these situations. They may often be asked to
  simulate a role that they are never likely to adopt in real life,

such as that of a detective or waiter. This does not mean that the language they practise in that role is of no value. Nonetheless, each learner should be allocated a fair proportion of roles which are more directly relevant in *one or both* of two senses: (a) he might reasonably expect to have to perform that role in foreign language situations outside the classroom; (b) he is already familiar with the role in his native language.

It is with these roles that learners are likely to identify most deeply. Through them, therefore, they have the greatest chance of relating to the foreign language with their whole personality, rather than merely manipulating it as an instrument which is external to them.

In chapters 7 and 8 we will consider some further points relevant to the activities discussed in this chapter and the preceding ones. In the meantime, I propose to look at a special category of communicative activity: listening activities.

6 Listening activities

6.1 Introduction

Most learners will spend considerably more time in listening to the foreign language than in producing it themselves. It is not only that they must understand what is said to them during face-to-face interaction. There is also a vast range of situations where they will be the silent receivers of messages directed at them, from radio, television, announcements and a multitude of other sources. In the foreign environment, the ability to make sense of these messages is often crucial for survival, as well as providing access to wider and richer experiences. In their own country, too, many learners will have more opportunities to hear the foreign language than to speak it.

When speaking, it is the learner himself who selects the language that is used. To some extent, therefore, he can compensate for deficiencies in his repertoire, through communicative strategies such as using paraphrase or simplifying his message. When listening, however, he cannot normally exercise any control over the language that is used: he must be prepared to extract meanings, as best he can, from whatever language is directed at him. It is therefore not enough that he should merely be able to understand the same range of language that he can speak: his receptive repertoire must be matched not against his own productive repertoire, but against the productive repertoire of the native speakers he will need to understand. In addition, he must be prepared to cope with a wide range of situational and performance factors which are outside his control. In particular:
- he will need to understand speech in situations where communication is made difficult by physical factors such as background noise, distance or unclear sound reproduction (e.g. over loudspeakers at airports or stations);
- he must become accustomed to speech which is not perfectly planned, but contains the false starts, hesitations and so on which characterise most everyday speech;
- he will need to understand speakers who vary in tempo of speech, clarity of articulation and regional accent. Especially where English is concerned, these will include other non-native speakers of the language.

Teachers now have access to an ever-increasing selection of recorded and broadcast materials. They can therefore plan a systematic extension of their learners' repertoire and skills, by exposing them to speech with varying linguistic and situational characteristics. This chapter will be concerned with what learners might be asked to *do* with such materials, since mere unmotivated exposure is not enough to ensure that they develop the ability to listen and understand. This will become clearer from the next section, which will discuss briefly the nature of listening comprehension.

6.2 The active nature of listening comprehension

Listening has often been called a passive skill. This is misleading, because listening demands active involvement from the hearer. In order to reconstruct the message that the speaker intends, the hearer must actively contribute knowledge from both linguistic and nonlinguistic sources. For example, it is only by applying his knowledge of the language that he can divide the continuous stream of sound into meaningful units at all, and it is only by comparing these units with the shared knowledge between himself and the speaker that he can interpret their meaning. Thus, as we saw in chapter 1, a single word such as 'Ready?' might have the force of an invitation to come and eat in some situations, but a totally different meaning in others. Likewise, we saw that the communicative value of 'Why don't you close the door?' depends on the situation and social relationship. In fact, the majority of utterances that we hear in daily life could be conceived as carrying different meanings in different circumstances, and it is only because we are actively involved in the communication process that we are generally able to relate them to a single appropriate meaning.

In this process of constructing meanings, the listener relies to varying degrees on individual linguistic signals. For example, let us say that he overhears somebody saying that 'Mr Smith bought a goat at the market yesterday'. If the listener has no previous knowledge of the event, most of the individual items carry new information which is relevant to the message: that it was *Mr* (not Mrs) *Smith* (not Jones) who *bought* (not sold) a *goat* (not a coat), and so on. There are therefore several points where, if the listener failed to process the linguistic signals (e.g. because of noise or inattention), he would also fail to extract the meaning. Normally, however, there is a higher level of 'redundancy' in speech, so that the listener does not need to process every single item. This would be the case if the preceding conversation had already established that Mr Smith had been to the market on the previous day. It would also be the case if somebody pointed to Mr Smith and said 'Look at that man! He's got a goat!': the utterance draws attention and communicates surprise, but otherwise carries no information that is not contained in the concrete situation. In the classroom, the teacher has a number of techniques at his disposal for increasing the redundancy of language and thus helping comprehension. For example, he might link the first utterance with a picture of a man and a goat. Alternatively, he might set up expectations by previously asking learners to listen for information about 'what Mr Smith bought at the market'.

The nature of listening comprehension means that the learner should be encouraged to engage in an active process of listening for meanings, using not only the linguistic cues but also his nonlinguistic knowledge. He should also be made aware that not every clue is equally important to the message. Therefore, even when he misses a piece of language, he need not panic: there is a good chance that other clues will enable him to understand the message, or at least, enough of the message for his own purpose. It may be, of course, that the missed item is one which radically alters the whole message. This does not affect the general point being made here, since the learner has more hope of realising his own misunderstanding if he stays involved in the communication, rather than letting himself be distracted by a sense of failure.

6.3 Listening with a purpose

The active nature of listening means that, no less than in speaking, the learner must be motivated by a communicative purpose. This purpose determines to a large extent what meanings he must listen for and which parts of the spoken text are most important to him. For example, there may be parts where he does not need to understand every detail, but only to listen for the general gist. There may be other parts where a topic of special significance arises, requiring him to listen for more detailed information – for example, so that he can report about the topic to other members of a group. At other times, a task may require him to listen for specific pieces of information distributed throughout the text.

The most familiar technique for providing a purpose for listening is, of course, by means of questions, which prompt learners to listen for specific facts or to make inferences from what they hear. If I do not discuss this technique here, it is not because I wish to dispute its value or convenience, but because it is already so widely familiar. I will therefore focus on other kinds of activity through which learners can be helped to develop their listening skills. Some of these activities will be similar to functional communication activities discussed in chapter 4, except that the learners must now achieve their purpose by listening not to each other, but to a third source (usually the teacher or a recording).

The activities will be grouped according to the kind of response that the learner must produce:
1 Performing physical tasks (e.g. selecting pictures).
2 Transferring information (e.g. into tabular form).
3 Reformulating and evaluating information.
The main emphasis will be on listening for *functional* information. However, we will also see that similar techniques can be used to motivate learners to listen for *social* meanings.

The nature of the learner's response is important for three main reasons. First, it is the need to produce an overt response that provides learners with their immediate motivation for listening. Second, it orients them towards certain kinds of meaning and thus helps them to structure their listening activity. Third, some kinds of response (notably the second category above) provide learners with a framework for conceptualising the central meanings of the text and for relating them to each other. However, this immediate response will not necessarily be the ultimate purpose of the listening. It may also serve as a preliminary to some other activity. For example, the information which learners obtain may serve as a basis for discussion, oral reports or writing. We saw in the last chapter (5.3), too, how a listening activity may form one component in an extended simulation exercise. Indeed, it is when the results of successful listening contribute to some further purpose that the learners are most strongly and realistically motivated.

Performing physical tasks

Through the activities described under this heading, the learner is alerted to look for specific meanings, related to a task which he must perform. This encourages him to listen selectively, extracting only information which is relevant to the task. In turn, this accustoms him to the idea that the criterion for success in listening is not whether he has understood every word, but whether he has constructed enough of the meanings in order to satisfy his own communicative purpose. In these activities, success is measured in a purely practical way: whether the nonlinguistic task is performed correctly or not.

Identification and selection

The learner has a set of pictures. These may be similar to the pictures used for the identification tasks described in chapter 4 (4.2). He must listen to a description or dialogue, and select the picture(s) which the spoken text refers to.

Alternatively, the learner may hold just one picture, and listen to two or three short descriptions or dialogues. He has to decide which spoken text refers to the picture.

In order to add interest, the task may be presented in various guises. For example, the learners may be asked to identify a wanted person or stolen car, described in a radio message. On another occasion, they may be asked to decide (on the basis of references within the text) which of two taped conversations took place in a particular setting or between two particular people. The decision may have to be reached through group discussion – an example of how the listening activity may lead to a different kind of language activity.

A well-known variant of the identification task is 'bingo'. Each learner has a card which depicts about nine or twelve items (e.g. numbers, objects, people or actions). The items have been chosen from a larger set of, say, thirty items. If possible, every card should depict a different selection from this set. However, the activity can also be organised on an impromptu basis by asking each learner to make his own selection from the total set and to enter the items on his card. The teacher then calls out items from the larger set. Alternatively, the learners may hear a description or dialogue in which they are mentioned. As he hears items that are on his own card, each learner must cross them off or cover them. The 'winner' is the first learner to cross off or cover all the items on his card.

From these examples, it is clear that the actual process of identification may involve varying degrees of complexity. At its simplest, it may be a question of just listening to a sequence of direct references to objects. At the other extreme, learners may have to listen to a continuous spoken text, in order to extract clues which link it to a specific situation or person.

Sequencing

This is a variation of the type of activity just described. Learners must now identify *successive* pictures that are described or mentioned, in order to place them in their correct sequence.

Again, the activity may be motivated by presenting it in various guises. For example, the pictures may represent the events in a story which learners listen to. Alternatively, they could represent the places visited by a group of tourists – the spoken text could either be in the form of a narrative, or it could consist of excerpts from conversations between the tourists as they view the different places.

Locating

A further variation is that learners are required to place items not into a sequence, but into their appropriate location, e.g. on a plan of a house or town. Alternatively, they may have to follow a route on a map.

As with other activities, the nature of the language input can vary. For example, it may consist of direct instructions which learners have to carry out; a spoken description of a scene; a conversation between two people who are discussing where to put furniture in a room or telling others about a recent journey; and so on.

Drawing and constructing

Learners are asked to listen to a description or discussion, and draw the scene (or plan of a house, etc.) which is described or referred to. They may first be provided with an outline which they have to complete, or a line drawing which they have to colour.

A variant is that learners have to construct a model or pattern, using blocks or pieces that are provided.

Performing other actions

Learners may be required to perform or mime other actions, as instructed or described.

In all of the activities described above, the focus has been on a practical result. The teacher can control how much of the linguistic input has to be processed by the learners, in order to achieve this result. At one extreme, it may be necessary to process every word, e.g. in order to follow precise instructions. At the other extreme, it may be necessary to scan the spoken text in order to extract a small number of relevant meanings, e.g. to identify which objects are mentioned in the course of a dialogue. In the second case, the overall complexity of the language might be far beyond what learners could normally cope with, since much of it is redundant to their immediate purpose: the level of difficulty depends above all on how accessible and prominent the *task-relevant* meanings are.

By varying the nature of the task between these two extremes, the teacher can accustom the learners to adapting their listening strategy to suit the immediate task.

Transferring information

In the activities included under this heading, learners are still required to look for specific types of meaning. It is also still the case that these meanings may be contained in a short text that has to be processed intensively, or a longer text that has to be scanned. Now, however, the outcome of the listening is no longer a physical response to the language. Learners must now extract relevant information from the text in order to transfer it to some other form, such as a table, chart or diagram. This structures and motivates the listening activity. It also creates expectations as to what meanings will occur in the spoken text, thus helping the learner to gain access to these meanings.

For example, in one of the activities in *Communicate,* learners are told that they will hear descriptions of five people:

A girl describing her fiancé.
A boy describing a girl he dislikes.
A writer describing a historical figure.
A police description of a criminal.
A friend describing his cousin whom you are going to meet.

They are provided with the following table:

	Hair	Build	Height	
1 Criminal				
2				
3				
4				
5				

As the learners listen to each description, they must first identify which person is being described, then fill in as much information as possible on the table. Here are two of the descriptions:

– He is 37 years old, approximately 5 ft 8 in tall with short black hair. He is well-built and extremely strong. This man is danger-

ous and may attack without warning. He should not be approached by members of the public.
– She'll be at the station at 5.30. She's got long red hair and she's very good-looking. She's fairly tall – about 5 ft 8 in and very slim. Yes, I'm sure you'll enjoy meeting her.

As a further example, learners may be asked to listen to a series of station announcements (authentic or simulated), and to record important details of trains:

Destination	Time of Departure	Platform	Calling at
Bristol			
		8	
	13.17		

One of the announcements could be:

The train now standing at platform 5 is the 12.35 to Bristol, calling at Cheltenham and Gloucester. Passengers for Cardiff should change at Gloucester.

The spoken text may be in the form of a conversation, which the learners 'overhear'. For example, in an activity in *Starting Strategies,* learners listen to a conversation in a restaurant car on a train. They have to write down what each speaker decides to eat and drink. In another activity, learners hear a number of interviews about journeys to work, and have to fill in a 'survey' form with the information given by speakers, about method of transport, distance, time and cost.

When the learners hear only one text, the type of table shown above may not be the most convenient way of setting out the information that is to be obtained. They may therefore be provided with a simpler framework indicating the facts they must listen for. For example, when listening to an interview, they may be asked to fill in an 'application form' with the personal details of the interviewee. When listening to a talk about a town, they may be asked to fill in a 'profile' with relevant facts, or perhaps to answer a series of true-or-false questions. Learners may even be asked simply to complete blanks in a number of statements. Other possibilities will suggest themselves as suitable for specific texts which the teacher wants to use.

In activities such as the ones described, learners can be given varying amounts of help by the table (or other framework) which the teacher provides. For example, in listening to the descriptions of people, they were prompted to look for certain specific facts about their hair, build, and so on. This narrowed down considerably the range of meanings that they would expect to hear; these clear expectations would make the comprehension task easier. However, as learners gain in independence, the teacher can make this preparatory guidance less detailed. For example, they may be asked to record three important facts about each person. Later, the instruction may be simply to make notes about the persons described in a similar series of texts. In this way, the teacher can gradually make the learners less dependent on outside help, and more capable of structuring their own listening.

The information that learners obtain in these activities often provides a particularly convenient basis for further language activity. For example, after listening to descriptions, learners may be asked to compose written portraits of the people described, perhaps also of people known to them. After listening to interviews, they may be asked to interview each other to obtain similar information. In *Listening Links* the materials are based on a useful technique for exploiting information obtained through listening as a stimulus for communicative interaction. The authors call it 'jigsaw listening'. For this, the class is divided into groups. Each group hears one of three different spoken texts. All texts deal with the same topic, but contain incomplete information. After obtaining the information from their own text, learners must exchange information with members of the other two groups. Between them, the texts have given the learners all the information which they need in order to solve some problem or piece together a complete account of some event. In other words, the listening provides the input for communicative activities of the kind discussed in chapter 4. At the same time, of course, the prospect of taking part in communicative interaction provides learners with a strong purpose for listening.

Reformulating and evaluating information

We saw above how the teacher can gradually decrease the specific preparation which he gives the learners as to what meanings they should expect or seek in the spoken text. He can do this to the point where the preparation he gives is minimal, perhaps little more than an indication of the topic of the text they are to hear. The learners themselves are responsible for extracting and structuring the main content of the text.

The teacher may now decide to give learners a more global task, oriented towards the text as a whole. For example, a natural development of the information-transfer activities discussed above is that learners should be asked to reformulate the important content in their own words, in the form of notes or a summary. Alternatively, learners may be required to evaluate the information contained in the spoken text, which may thus serve as a stimulus for written argument or group discussion. Again, these activities may be further motivated by their function in a broader context of activity, such as a role-playing exercise.

6.4 Listening for social meaning

In discussing listening activities in this chapter, we have assumed that learners will be listening for the *functional* meanings expressed in the spoken text. However, as we saw in chapter 1, it is also important that learners should develop an awareness of the *social* implications of language forms. Some of the activities which I have described can be adapted so that they require learners to focus on social aspects of language use.

For example, in a previous section (6.3) I mentioned that learners could be asked to match conversations with situations shown in pictures. The assumption was that the *content* of the speech would provide the necessary clues. However, the clues could be provided not so much by the content as by the *forms* which the speakers select. Thus, after hearing two short extracts in which people greet each other with different degrees of formality, learners might be asked to match them with two situations in which other clues (e.g. dress, posture) also suggest different degrees of formality. Since many of the features relevant to social meaning cannot be presented visually, the teacher may prefer to provide a verbal outline of the situation and the relationship between the people. It is important, however, to avoid creating stereotypes in learners' minds ('rich ladies always talk like that', 'if he says that, he must be a student', and so on). Rather, it is necessary to stress that social appropriacy is a fluid quality, without black and white distinctions.

This last point is brought out more clearly by the kind of activity contained in *Variations on a Theme*. Learners hear short extracts from dialogues, without being told who the speakers are or what the situation is. They must then interpret and discuss the dialogues, expressing their ideas on such matters as who the speakers might be, how long they have known each other, what the situation is, what the speakers' mood is, and so on. The learners are not given clear-cut answers to these questions. The excerpts can therefore stimulate open-ended discussion and problem-solving, of the kind discussed in chapter 4 (4.5) and chapter 5(5.2).

6.5 Summary

In this chapter, we have seen a number of activities which involve learners in listening with a specific purpose. This purpose is based on the need to produce some sort of response (linguistic or otherwise) to the spoken text. We have also seen, in several instances, how the listening activity can provide the input for further language activity, such as writing or discussion.

We should remember again that in order to accustom the learners gradually to an increasing range of speech, the teacher can vary a number of factors in the spoken text itself. These include:
– Linguistic factors such as complexity and degree of formality.
– Performance factors such as accent, speed, fluency and clarity.
– Situational factors such as background noise and acoustic conditions.
– The type of text, e.g. dialogues, reports, descriptions, instructions.
In addition to these factors which relate to the spoken text, the teacher can also control two pedagogical factors of particular importance:
– The extent to which nonlinguistic information (e.g. from pictures) helps learners to interpret the text.
– The proportion of the total number of linguistic signals that the learners must process, in order to carry out the task before them.
The emphasis in the discussion has been on activities where the communicative purpose is practical, rather than simple interest or curiosity. This is not meant to imply that listening for interest is not valuable as an activity and as a goal. However, it depends on the learner being individually motivated by the content of the listening material. It is therefore difficult to control in a way that enables us to help learners develop their skills by a gradual progression. Listening for interest is probably best organized, whenever possible, in a way that allows the learner to select his listening material for himself and match his listening strategy to his own needs. On the other hand, we can provide more systematic opportunities for *developing* these strategies when we control the learner's listening by means of specific goals which depend on it.

7 Choosing what to teach

7.1 Introduction

Throughout the book, the emphasis has been on methodology rather than content – on *how* to teach rather than *what* to teach. In the present chapter, however, I propose to look briefly at this second aspect of communicative language teaching. It has been the subject of much discussion and controversy since the early 1970s, under headings such as 'communicative', 'functional' or 'notional' syllabus design. Here, I do not propose to go deeply into the issues, many of which are of more interest to the course-writer than to the teacher. I will restrict myself to considering how:
- a communicative view of language can help the teacher to make the linguistic content of a course more relevant to learners' needs;
- a communicative view of language can provide the teacher with alternative ways of organising this content into teaching units (e.g. lessons or sequences of lessons).

These questions are not only relevant to the teacher designing his own course. Even when the teacher is using a published course, he has to consider whether it should be adapted or complemented, so that it will be more suited to his learners' needs. In addition, every teacher has to decide what language, topics or situations he should include in the additional practice activities that he devises.

7.2 Choosing course-content

It is perfectly possible, of course, to select and organise the content of a course without any reference at all to what the learners will want to do with the language. Many grammar-translation textbooks, for example, take a structural analysis of the language as their sole frame of reference. They introduce the learner systematically to the basic structures, grading these from simple to complex, so that the learner can steadily increase his mastery of the linguistic system. In its extreme form, this approach can present learners with communicatively useless pieces of language which have been selected only because they exemplify certain grammatical facts. A much quoted example is the notorious 'My grandmother's eartrumpet has been struck by lightning'. This is an excellent illustration of the passive construction, but remote in meaning from anything that the learners might need to say themselves.

A communicative approach to the content of a course need not involve abandoning the use of structural criteria for selection and sequencing. As I emphasised in chapter 1, mastery of the structural system is still the basic requirement for using language to communicate one's own meanings. However, as we also saw in chapter 1, a communicative approach encourages us to go beyond structures and take account of other aspects of communication. It can therefore help us to match the content more closely with the actual communicative uses that the learners will have to make of the foreign language. For example:

– When deciding which linguistic forms and distinctions should be emphasised in the limited time available, the teacher can give priority to those which seem to offer the greatest value in widening the learners' communicative repertoire. For example, 'can + infinitive' enables them to express a number of important communicative functions, so that the teacher may deal with the pattern intensively from an early stage. On the other hand, it is less urgent that they should distinguish between 'I will' and 'I shall', since this is rarely (if ever) necessary for effective communication. At a later stage, 'he should have (seen it)' increases the range of meanings that the learners can express, whereas 'he might have (seen it)' only duplicates what they can probably say already with 'perhaps he (saw it)'.

On the basis of their communicative value for the learner, the teacher will often draw a distinction between forms that the learners should master for productive use and those which they need only recognise for comprehension purposes.

– When introducing and practising structures, the teacher can do this through language that reflects as closely as possible the topics that the learners might want to talk about. To use an example mentioned earlier, they are never likely to want to say that 'grandmother's eartrumpet has been struck by lightning'. However, they might need to say that 'John's car has been towed away by the police', or some similar utterance using the passive construction.

This is, of course, merely a repetition of the familiar principle that students learn better if they practise the foreign language through vocabulary and topics that are relevant to their interests. Such practice is not only more efficient in terms of their learning goals, but also more motivating. Nonetheless, because of the nature of the classroom, there may be occasions when the learners can develop communicative skills by using language which is apparently irrelevant to their later needs (e.g. by describing patterns or talking about classroom objects).

- In controlled activities such as those discussed in chapter 2, the teacher can attempt to relate the language practice to communicative functions which learners might need to express. For example, practice of 'can + infinitive' may be related to asking permission, 'where's the . . . ?' may be related to asking directions, and so on. When structures are 're-cycled' for further treatment or revision, they might be related to different functions (e.g. talking about ability with 'can', seeking information with 'where's the . . . ?').

  Working from the other direction, the teacher can use a check-list of important communicative functions (see section 7.4 below) and make sure that, at some time during their course, the learners practise ways of expressing them all. As with other aspects of language, he will often wish the learners to understand a wider range of possible expressions than they can produce themselves.

- In devising more creative activities such as those discussed in chapters 4 and 5, the teacher can also take account of learners' probable needs. For example, in discussion and problem-solving activities, he can include topics which reflect the learner's interests. In role-playing activities, he can include situations and topics which the learners might expect to encounter outside the classroom.

  As with communicative functions, the teacher can also work from the other direction. Using a check-list of important topics and situations, he can attempt to expose the learner to as many as possible of them at some time during the course.

This section has indicated some of the ways in which a communicative approach can help the teacher to make the content of a course reflect not only the structural demands of the foreign language, but also some of the more specific communicative demands which learners might need to cope with. However, we should not forget that the exact nature of these demands is unpredictable, since they depend on the uncertainties of everyday life and communication. The learner's ability to negotiate these uncertainties depends only partly on whether we have exposed him to particular pieces of relevant language (e.g. vocabulary). More than this, it depends on whether he has developed a creative ability to use the foreign grammatical system for communicating new meanings in unpredicted situations. In trying to predict and cater for specific needs, we should not be led to neglect this fundamental aspect of communicative ability.

7.3 Organising course-content

In the previous section, I mentioned some ways in which a communicative view of language can help us to make the content of a course more relevant to learners' needs. In doing so, I assumed that the basic organisation of the course would be based on the structures of the language. In the present section, I will look at other possibilities, based on other aspects of language use. The aim is not to be exhaustive, but rather to illustrate that these alternative frameworks for courses exist. The teacher is increasingly likely to come across such alternatives in published courses and may decide to adopt them himself when planning lessons.

Functional-structural organisation

Without actually abandoning structural grading of the language that is taught, a course may be organised into units based on important communicative functions. The learners then progress from function to function rather than from structural pattern to structural pattern. However, the linguistic forms for the different functions are at first kept simple, and the sequencing of the functions is carefully adapted, so that the learner still works through a graded structural progression.

An example of this form of organisation is *Starting Strategies*. If we look at the first seven units of this course, we see that the learner is presented with sequences of communicative functions rather than structural patterns. These functions include 'asking somebody's name', 'asking and saying where places are', 'saying what somebody's job is' and 'talking about nationality'. However, the language through which the learner is required to express these functions is based almost exclusively on simple structural patterns with parts of 'to be' in the present tense, e.g. 'What's your name?', 'Where's Kent Road?', 'Is Sally a journalist? – Yes, she is', 'Are they English? – No, they aren't'. Unlike most courses organised around structural categories, however, the verb 'to be' is never presented as a teaching point in its own right, independent of specific communicative functions.

In the previous section, I mentioned how, with a structure-based course, the teacher can 're-cycle' structures in relation to new functions. In a similar way, with a functional-structural form of organisation, the teacher can re-cycle *functions,* each time with more complex language to suit the learners' developing linguistic competence. For example, 'asking directions' might first be expressed by 'Where's the station, please?', later by 'Can you tell me the way to the station, please?', and later still by 'Excuse me, I wonder if you could direct me to the station?'. By this time, of course, the learners must also be made aware of the *social* meaning of alternative forms.

Functional organisation

With the type of organisation just discussed, we assumed that the learners were still engaged in acquiring the basic structural patterns of the language. Therefore, it was necessary to keep some form of structural progression in the organisation of the course (claims that this can be dispensed with have not so far been proven). However, with learners who have already acquired the basic structures of the language, the teacher can consider going over to a form of organisation that reflects directly the potential *communicative uses* of the foreign language. One way of doing this is to base the units of the course on important communicative functions.

This is the form of organisation adopted by *Functions of English.* Each teaching unit is based on a group of communicative functions (e.g. 'Offering, asking permission, giving reasons'). Each function is represented by a range of linguistic forms, chosen on the grounds of their communicative usefulness and social appropriacy rather than for their structural make-up. Language of widely varying grammatical complexity is thus grouped together for functional reasons. For example, the expressions which are suggested for asking permission include the simple 'I'd like to leave early' together with the complex 'I hope you don't mind, but would it be at all possible for me to leave early?'. Because the course is not based on any kind of structural progression, the units can be dealt with in any sequence.

Notional organisation

Another possibility with more advanced learners is to organise units around the 'notions' that learners should be able to express. In discussing syllabuses, the term 'notion' usually refers to general concepts such as 'quantity', 'cause' or 'time'. Thus, units could be based on, say, different ways of expressing causal relationships or quantity.

Vital English, for example, is divided into a number of large units organised around notions (e.g. 'quantity and degree'). Most of the practice activities in *Vital English* are of a controlled kind (e.g. traditional drills). A notion-based course in which the activities are more creative and communicative is *Notions in English.* Unit 10, for example, presents various ways of expressing 'future time' and engages learners in a variety of activities where they themselves must talk about future events.

Topic-based organisation

Another aspect of communicative language use which can provide a framework for a course is the topics that learners need to be prepared to deal with. The teacher can take an important area of meanings such as sport or politics and within this area, he can present useful language and engage the learners in a variety of practice activities.

An example of this form of organisation is *English Topics.* The units of the course are based on ten topics (teaching, holidays, the supernatural, houses, food, speech, jobs, sports and games, fashion and pop, and the arts). Each unit presents language and includes various activities related to its topic area. The activities include reading, listening comprehension, discussion and role-playing.

Other alternatives

It is not necessary to opt for only one form of organisation for a course, as there are several ways in which different organisational principles can be combined. For example:
– Different forms of organisation can be 'nested' inside each other. This is the case with *Vital English* which was used as an example of notional course organisation above. Each of the large 'notional' units is in fact divided into smaller units based on different topics (e.g. 'health'). Within each smaller unit the practice activities focus on specific communicative functions (e.g. 'enquiring about obligation'). The combination of the notion 'quantity' with the topic 'health' and the function 'enquiring about obligation' produces practice items such as 'Do I have to take a half or a whole teaspoonful?'.
  Similarly, an individual teacher could take a broad topic area such as 'travel' and focus on a number of communicative functions within that area (e.g. ways of asking directions, asking for information about trains, discussing preferences, and so on).

81

– It is possible to use different kinds of organisation as a basis
for different units, according to which perspective offers the
most convenient way of approaching a particular area of
language. For example, while *Notions in English* bases many
of its units on ways of expressing notions such as 'motion' or
'place', others are organised around topics such as 'politics' or
'shops' and others around grammatical categories such as 'passive' or 'gerunds and infinitives'.
– While learners are still working within a mainly structure-
based progression, the teacher may sometimes insert a unit
which is organised around an aspect of communicative use.
For example, let us say that the students have reached a stage
in the progression where they have learnt a number of grammatical patterns which can express the function 'asking permission'. At this point, the teacher may decide to focus on
that particular function, gathering together and practising the
various ways of expressing it. This principle could be extended
so that, after the initial stages, there is a function-based syllabus running parallel to the structural progression.

There is little firm evidence about the comparative effectiveness
of the alternative forms of organisation. As so often, much will
depend on the individual teacher's preferences, as well as those of
different learners. For the forms of organisation based on aspects
of communicative use, we can point to the clear advantage (for
both learners and teachers) that they help to ensure a constant
link between language learning and the students' communicative
goals.

7.4 Check-lists for predicting communicative needs

In deciding what functions, topics and so on are most likely to
be relevant to the learners' needs, teachers must rely ultimately
on their own intuition and observation. However, they can make
their task easier by using published check-lists, which they can
modify as they think necessary.

A document which has proved particularly valuable for this
purpose is the Council of Europe's 'Threshold Level.' This is an
attempt to specify (a) the most important communicative needs
that are likely to arise in everyday situations and (b) suitable
language forms that could be learnt for coping with these needs.
It assumes a 'general' learner who wants to cross the 'threshold'
into a reasonably normal life in the foreign country, or who

wants to interact with foreign visitors in his own country. About
this learner, it helps the teacher to answer questions such as:

1 What *situations* might the learner encounter?
   The specification lists some of the situations in which the
   learner is most likely to need to use the foreign language.
   These include 'transactional' situations in which the language is
   predictable to some extent (e.g. in a bank or a supermarket).
   In other situations (e.g. personal conversations with friends), a
   vast range of different linguistic needs could arise.

2 What *language activities* is the learner most likely to take part
   in?
   The specification assumes that the learner will need to participate mostly in oral language activities. He will only have limited needs in writing and reading. It recognises, however, that
   these latter activities may still have an important methodological function as an aid to learning.

3 What *functions* of language are likely to be most useful?
   The specification lists 68 communicative functions which it
   considers to be most important. Some of these are comparatively 'small-scale' and may be expressed by conventionalised
   forms (e.g. accepting an invitation). Others (e.g. describing
   and narrating) are much more extensive, and the actual language needed will be determined almost entirely by the topics
   and notions involved.

4 What *topics* are likely to be important?
   The specification gives a list of topic-areas that might be important. For each topic, it suggests what the students should
   be able to do with it (e.g. sports: state own preferences, etc.),
   thus linking topics with communicative functions. It also lists
   important 'topic-related notions' (e.g. under sports: team, to
   play, game, race, to swim, etc.). These will determine, to a
   large extent, what specific items of vocabulary the learners will
   need.

5 What *general notions* are likely to be important?
   The specification provides a list of general notions such as
   location, number, ownership etc., which the learners might need
   to express.

Up to this point, the specification has applied equally to learners
of any foreign language for general purposes: it is a prediction of
communicative needs, and these needs would be expressed in whatever language the students happened to be learning. Indeed, a
major aim of the document is to specify equivalent communicative objectives for learners of different foreign languages. From
now, however, the document we are discussing refers specifically

to English. There are other documents which relate to other languages.

6 What *language forms* should the students learn, in order to satisfy the communicative needs that have been described?

The Threshold Level lists these under three main headings: forms which express *communicative functions* (mostly grammatical patterns); forms which express *general notions* (grammatical patterns and items of vocabulary); and forms which express *topic-related notions* (mostly items of vocabulary). It distinguishes between forms which should be mastered for productive use and forms which need to be mastered for comprehension purposes only. Where necessary, especially for productive use, it recognises the importance of structural factors in language learning by selecting the simplest way of expressing a function or notion.

The language forms contained in these lists are also presented from three other perspectives: as a list of words, as a structural inventory, and as a grammatical summary.

The various lists of the Threshold Level provide a tentative description of the general learner's communicative needs and of the language needed for satisfying them. They also offer a model procedure which teachers can follow themselves if they wish to carry out their own assessment of their learners' needs. Any such assessment cannot be other than approximate, of course, so that we must again remember what I emphasised earlier in the chapter (7.2): however much we try to match content with communicative needs, the learners will only be able to communicate successfully in everyday situations if we help them towards a communicative ability which is sufficiently flexible and creative to *go beyond* the needs we have predicted.

7.5 Summary

In this chapter, we have seen some ways in which the teacher can take account of communicative aspects of language and language use, in order to choose content which is likely to be relevant to his learners' needs. We have also seen how these factors can suggest alternative ways of organising this content into teaching units. Finally, we have looked briefly at one document which teachers can use (or a procedure which they can follow) when deciding what the learners' needs are most likely to be.

8 A communicative approach

8.1 Introduction

This concluding chapter will move aside from the discussion of specific learning activities which has been the main concern of this book. It will look at a number of more general factors which, together, contribute towards an overall communicative approach to foreign language teaching. First, it will summarise the conceptual and methodological framework which the book has used. It will then point out some ways in which this framework might help the teacher to orient his own activity within the classroom. Finally, it will consider how certain psychological factors in the classroom might help or hinder the learners in their acquisition of communicative ability.

8.2 Methodological framework

The most important methodological distinction used in this book has been that between pre-communicative and communicative learning activities. The distinction may be summarised as follows:

1 Through *pre-communicative* activities, the teacher isolates specific elements of knowledge or skill which compose communicative ability, and provides the learners with opportunities to practise them separately. The learners are thus being trained in the part-skills of communication rather than practising the total skill to be acquired.

This category includes the majority of the learning activities currently to be found in textbooks and methodological handbooks, such as different types of drill or question-and-answer practice. These aim above all to provide learners with a fluent command of the linguistic system, without actually requiring them to use this system for communicative purposes. Accordingly, the learners' main purpose is to produce language which is acceptable (i.e. sufficiently accurate or appropriate) rather than to communicate meanings effectively.

In chapter 2 we saw how some of these activities, more than others, attempt to create links between the language forms being practised and their potential functional meanings. These activities can be subcategorised as 'quasi-communicative', because they take account of communicative as well as structural facts about language, in contrast with purely structural activities such as performing mechanical drills or learning verb paradigms.

2 In *communicative* activities, the learner has to activate and integrate his pre-communicative knowledge and skills, in order to use them for the communication of meanings. He is therefore now engaged in practising the total skill of communication. However, as we saw in chapters 4 and 5, there is still immense variation in the demands that may be posed by different types of communication situation.

Here again, it is convenient to distinguish two subcategories, depending now on the degree of importance attached to social as well as functional meaning. In what we have called 'functional communication activities', the learner is placed in a situation where he must perform a task by communicating as best he can, with whatever resources he has available. The criterion for success is practical: how effectively the task is performed. In 'social interaction activities', on the other hand, the learner is also encouraged to take account of the social context in which communication takes place. He is required to go beyond what is necessary for simply 'getting meanings across', in order to develop greater social acceptability in the language he uses. In the first instance, this may simply mean greater grammatical accuracy; later, it may also involve producing speech which is socially appropriate to specific situations and relationships.

This methodological framework can be represented diagrammatically as follows:

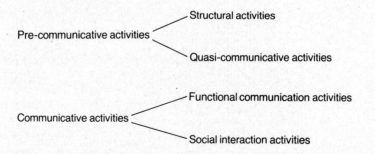

There is no clear dividing line in reality between these different categories and subcategories: they represent differences of emphasis and orientation rather than distinct divisions. We saw this in connection with cued dialogues, which were discussed both as a pre-communicative activity (in chapter 2) and as a communicative activity (in chapter 5). Similarly, it would be arbitrary if we tried to specify how much attention must be paid to communicative function before an activity can be called quasi-communicative, or how significant social meaning must become before it falls into the social interaction subcategory. In any case, in the last resort these distinctions depend on the varying orientations of individual learners. For example, during question-and-answer practice about personal background ('Where do you live?' etc.), it is possible that some learners will focus primarily on the meanings that are being conveyed, while others in the same group focus more strongly on the linguistic forms that are being used. If we tried to apply the above categories literally, we would need to say that the activity is communicative for the first learners, but pre-communicative for the second.

8.3 Sequencing of pre-communicative and communicative work

The layout of the diagram in the previous section is intended to show the *methodological relationship* between different types of activity. It does not necessarily show the *temporal sequencing* of such activities within a teaching unit.

Whenever pre-communicative activities occur, their essential function is a subordinate one: they serve to prepare the learner for later communication. Many teachers will wish most of their teaching sequences to reflect this relationship directly. That is, they will begin a teaching unit (e.g. a lesson or series of lessons) with pre-communicative activities in which the learners practise certain language forms or functions. These activities will lead into communicative work, during which the learners can use the new language they have acquired and the teacher can monitor their progress. In effect, this is the familiar progression from 'controlled practice' to 'creative language use'.

However, it is also possible to reverse this sequence. That is, the teacher may *begin* a teaching unit with a communicative activity, such as a role-play based on a situation which the learners might expect to encounter. In addition to its intrinsic value as communication practice, this activity performs two other functions: it enables the teacher to diagnose the learners' weaknesses in a particular kind of communication situation, and it enables the learners themselves to become aware of their language needs. On the basis of his own diagnosis and perhaps after discussion with the learners, the teacher can organise controlled practice of language forms which would have enabled the learners to communicate more effectively or appropriately. There will then be a further phase of communicative activity, in which the learners can apply their new linguistic knowledge and skills.

Especially with intermediate or more advanced learners, this second procedure may help to increase the efficiency of the course in covering actual deficiencies in the learners' repertoire. Also, to the extent that the learners see the initial activity as a true reflection of their goals – the teacher himself can explain how these are related, of course – they will also see more clearly the purpose of the subsequent pre-communicative activities, with obvious advantages for their motivation. (We can continue to describe the activities as *pre*-communicative, since their function is still to *prepare* the learners for their future communication.) However, the second procedure obviously means that the teacher must dispense with using a planned syllabus. An exception to this is if he uses the initial communicative activity not for genuine diagnostic purposes, but only as a device for convincing learners of the necessity of language which he intends them to practise in any case.

Otherwise, the main purpose of the framework presented in the previous section is to suggest a way of integrating various activities into a coherent methodology, irrespective of how these activities are grouped into actual lessons or other units. At this level, in any case, the teacher's decisions have to take account not only of methodological considerations, but also of situation-specific factors which lie outside the scope of the present discussion (for example, the learners' motivation and concentration span, the frequency and length of timetabled lessons, or the availability of facilities and materials).

8.4   Focus on form and focus on meaning

At several points in the book, I have indicated the most important variable in the methodological framework summarised above. It is the varying degree to which the different activities encourage learners to focus on (a) linguistic forms to be practised, or (b) meanings to be conveyed.

In our everyday language use, we normally focus our attention primarily on the *meaning* of what we say or hear, rather than on its linguistic form. For example, if we are asked to recall what another person said, we can often remember the message, but not the exact words that were used. Similarly, in speaking, we make conscious decisions about the messages we want to convey, but the lower-level choices of structure and vocabulary occur more or less automatically. However, the actual degree of automaticity varies in relation to factors such as the complexity of the message to be conveyed, the familiarity of the situation and, of course, the individual speaker's communicative ability. For every speaker, there comes a point where he must consciously search for words to express what he means, or consciously reflect on words in order to interpret what he has heard. This point naturally comes sooner when the speaker is performing through a foreign language.

From this perspective, we can define the goal of foreign language teaching in the following terms: to extend the range of communication situations in which the learner can perform with focus on meaning, without being hindered by the attention he must pay to linguistic form. In relation to this goal, the roles of the two main categories of activity can be summarised as follows:

1 Pre-communicative activities aim to give the learners fluent control over linguistic forms, so that the lower-level processes will be capable of unfolding automatically in response to higher-level decisions based on meanings. Although the activities may emphasise the links between forms and meanings, the main criterion for success is whether the learner produces acceptable language.

2 In communicative activities, the production of linguistic forms becomes subordinate to higher-level decisions, related to the communication of meanings. The learner is thus expected to increase his skill in starting from an intended meaning, selecting suitable language forms from his total repertoire, and producing them fluently. The criterion for success is whether the meaning is conveyed effectively.

Again we should remember that we are dealing not with clear-cut distinctions but with gradual changes of emphasis. In chapter 4, for example, we saw activities where the learner is required both to use structures specified by the teacher, and to communicate meanings for a purpose. In such activities, the focus might be distributed in equal proportion between the forms to be produced and the meanings to be conveyed. As we shall see in the next section, the teacher may reinforce this dual focus not only through his preparation and presentation of the activity, but also through the *feedback* he provides in response to the learners' performance.

8.5 Feedback

A particularly important factor in determining the learners' relative focus on linguistic forms and meanings is the nature of the feedback they receive.

Feedback provides learners with knowledge of how successful their performance has been. The concept of success is, however, not absolute: it is determined by the focus or purpose of an activity. Thus, if the purpose is to produce certain pre-determined linguistic structures, success will be measured according to correspondingly *structural* criteria, namely: how accurately and/or fluently the structures are produced. On the other hand, if the purpose is to convey or comprehend meanings, success will be measured according to *communicative* criteria, namely: how effectively communication takes place. As we saw at the end of the previous section, an activity may combine both purposes, to varying degrees. In this case, success will be measured according to both structural and communicative criteria.

Feedback, likewise, may focus on the level of form and/or meaning. Let us assume, for example, that a learner produces the utterance 'Where you went last night?'. He may be informed (e.g. by the teacher or by the correct version in a taped drill) that the correct form is 'Where *did you go* last night?'. This is *structural* (or 'formal') feedback, telling him how successful his performance was according to structural criteria. Alternatively (or perhaps, in addition), the same utterance may receive a response which relates not to its form but to its meaning, for example the answer 'I went to the cinema'. To the learner, this constitutes *communicative* feedback: it tells him that his utterance has been understood as he intended. Clearly, an utterance may be successful according to communicative criteria even though it is formally incorrect. Likewise, an utterance may be formally correct but fail to convey the intended meaning.

Since feedback carries information about how successful the learner has been, the nature of the feedback also tells the learner what *criteria* for success are operative during a particular activity, and therefore indicates what his own purpose and focus should be. For example, if the teacher consistently corrects linguistic forms, this indicates that success is now being measured by formal criteria, and that the learner should therefore focus his attention (partly or wholly) on the production of correct linguistic forms. On the other hand, when a teacher wants his learners to focus on the effective communication of meanings, he must reinforce this focus by providing them with feedback about how successful communication has been. In some activities, such as many of those in chapter 4, this feedback may be intrinsic to the task: successful completion of the task is itself an indication that communication has been effective. In others, such as most role-playing activities, the feedback is provided by the reactions of the teacher or (especially) of other learners – that is, their reactions to the *meanings* of utterances rather than to their linguistic form.

It is therefore important for the teacher to monitor the kind of feedback that his learners receive, from himself or from others, so that it supports the methodological purpose of the activity. For example:

- In pre-communicative activities, he will need to provide feedback relating to linguistic form. However, this does not necessarily exclude communicative feedback. For example, while he is drilling a new structure through question-and-answer practice, a teacher may react to the meanings of the learners' responses as well as to their formal accuracy. This can help to create the illusion of a 'communicative' exchange and thus reinforce the links between structure and meaning.
- In communicative activities, the teacher will need to provide communicative feedback. Again, this need not exclude structural feedback altogether. However, the teacher must be aware that excessive correction will encourage learners to shift their focus from meanings to forms. For this reason, as we saw in chapters 4 and 5, he may often withhold structural correction, or postpone it until after the activity.

8.6 The role of the teacher

In the previous section, as at various other points in the book, I indicated that a teacher might decide not to correct errors that he observes. To many teachers, this might appear to conflict with their pedagogical role, which has traditionally required them to evaluate all learners' performance according to clearly defined criteria. Certainly, it suggests that a communicative approach involves the teacher in redefining, to some extent, this traditional role.

One of the most obvious features about the development of communicative ability (so obvious, indeed, that it can easily be ignored) is that it occurs through processes *inside the learner*. The teacher can offer the kinds of stimulus and experience that these processes seem to require, but has no direct control over them. There is evidence, in fact, that whatever the teacher does to influence the course of development, the learner will attempt to follow a sequence of learning determined by his own natural processes (or 'internal syllabus'). If we look at foreign language learning as it occurs in the natural environment, it also becomes clear that these processes can work without any teacher at all, so long as the environment provides the necessary stimuli and experience. The most essential of these seems to be that the learner should need to use the foreign language for communicative purposes.

This does not mean that teachers are not necessary, because the classroom is not the natural environment: unless the language classroom is intentionally structured, it will not provide learners either with adequate exposure to the foreign language or with adequate motivation to communicate through it. However, the teacher must be prepared to subordinate his own behaviour to the learning needs of his students. This includes recognising that learning does not only take place as a direct result of his own instruction. There are some aspects of learning that can take place more efficiently if, once he has initiated an activity, he takes no further part in it, but leaves full scope to his students' spontaneous learning processes.

The concept of the teacher as 'instructor' is thus inadequate to describe his overall function. In a broad sense, he is a 'facilitator of learning', and may need to perform in a variety of specific roles, separately or simultaneously. These include the following:

- As general overseer of his students' learning, he must aim to coordinate the activities so that they form a coherent progression, leading towards greater communicative ability. For this, he may use the methodological framework summarised in this chapter.
- As classroom manager, he is responsible for grouping activities into 'lessons' and for ensuring that these are satisfactorily organised at the practical level. This includes deciding on his own role within each activity.
- In many activities, he may perform the familiar role of language instructor: he will present new language, exercise direct control over the learners' performance, evaluate and correct it, and so on.
- In others, he will not intervene after initiating the proceedings, but will let learning take place through independent activity. This will frequently be communicative activity, but may also be pre-communicative (e.g. the use of pair-work as in chapter 2).
- While such independent activity is in progress, he may act as consultant or adviser, helping where necessary. He may also

move about the classroom in order to monitor the strengths
and weaknesses of the learners, as a basis for planning future
learning activities.
- He will sometimes wish to participate in an activity as 'co-
communicator' with the learners. In this role, he can stimulate
and present new language, without taking the main initiative
for learning away from the learners themselves.

In only one of these roles, then, is he the traditional dominator
of the classroom interaction. This fact is significant not only for
methodological reasons, but also, as we shall see, for its effect on
human relationships within the classroom.

8.7 Psychological factors in the classroom

In the previous section, we noted that communicative ability de-
velops by processes internal to the learner. The conclusion we
drew from this is that the teacher must subordinate his teaching
behaviour to the learning needs of his students, sometimes even
to the extent of withdrawing completely from an activity once it
is in progress. In this section, we will draw another conclusion:
since the developmental processes occur inside the learner, a crucial factor in helping or hindering them is the learner's psychological state.

It is all too easy for a foreign language classroom to create inhibitions and anxiety. It is not uncommon to find a teaching situation where, for example:
- the learners remain constantly aware of their own state of ig-
norance before a teacher who possesses all relevant knowledge;
- they are expected to speak or act only in response to immediate stimuli or instructions from the teacher (or tape, etc.);
- whatever they say or do is scrutinised in detail, with every
shortcoming being made a focus for comment.

In such circumstances, the learners occupy a permanent position
of inferiority before a critical audience, with little opportunity
for asserting their own individuality. They are unlikely to feel
drawn out to communicate with those around them or to
develop positive attitudes towards their learning environment. On
the contrary, many learners will prefer to keep a 'low profile', in
the hope that they will not be called upon to participate openly.

The development of communicative skills can only take place
if learners have motivation and opportunity to express their own
identity and to relate with the people around them. It therefore
requires a learning atmosphere which gives them a sense of
security and value as individuals. In turn, this atmosphere

depends to a large extent on the existence of interpersonal relationships which do not create inhibitions, but are supportive and
accepting.

The encouragement of such relationships is an essential concern of a communicative approach to foreign language teaching.
Clearly, it is a concern which cannot be satisfied through methodology alone, since it involves a wide range of personality factors and interpersonal skills. However, the teacher is helped by a
number of important aspects of the activities discussed in this
book. For example:

- The teacher's role in the learning process is recognised as less
  dominant. More emphasis is placed on the learner's contribution through independent learning.
- The emphasis on communicative interaction provides more
  opportunities for cooperative relationships to emerge, both
  among learners and between teacher and learners.
- Communicative interaction gives learners more opportunities
  to express their own individuality in the classroom. It also
  helps them to integrate the foreign language with their own
  personality and thus to feel more emotionally secure with it.
- These points are reinforced by the large number of activities
  where the class is divided into groups or pairs, which interact
  independently of the teacher.
- The teacher's role as 'co-communicator' places him on an
  equal basis with the learners. This helps to break down tension
  and barriers between them.
- Learners are not being constantly corrected. Errors are
  regarded with greater tolerance, as a completely normal
  phenomenon in the development of communicative skills.

In short, communicative teaching methods leave the learner
scope to contribute his own personality to the learning process.
They also provide the teacher with scope to step out of his
didactic role in order to be a 'human among humans'.

8.8 Conclusion

Chapter 1 began the main discussion by reminding us that communicative ability is a complex and many-sided phenomenon. It
argued that foreign language teaching must broaden its scope to
take account of this fact. The chief concern of the book has been
to suggest ways in which this might come about.

The previous section ended the discussion by reminding us
that the individual learner, too, is a complex and many-sided
phenomenon. It argued that his individuality must be respected

and encouraged to find expression. Retrospectively, it suggested that many of the learning activities discussed in this book provide opportunities for this to take place.

The underlying message, then, is that foreign language teaching must be concerned with reality: with the reality of communication as it takes place outside the classroom and with the reality of learners as they exist outside and inside the classroom. Because both of these realities are so complex and poorly understood, nobody will ever produce a definitive teaching methodology. This book, like any other on the topic, is therefore no more than a small chapter in a story that has no end.

In the meantime, I hope that you can derive some practical use from it.

Further reading

In compiling this section and the bibliography that follows it, I have had to decide whether to offer a small number of general suggestions, so that readers could follow all of them if they wished, or a larger number of more specific suggestions, from which each reader could select whatever suited his or her purposes. I have chosen the second alternative. This means that the references are more numerous than I first intended, but I hope that, as a result, they will cater to a wider variety of readers' needs. In particular, I have tried to include a balanced selection of both (a) books and articles which take the reader further into the underlying principles of communicative language teaching and (b) books, articles and published materials which illustrate practical techniques.

In the present section, I refer only to author and date of publication. Fuller details are given in the bibliography. I have tried to include only material which is fairly widely distributed, but of course, many items will be more easily available in some parts of the world than in others.

Introduction

Some influential papers of the 1970s are reprinted in Brumfit and Johnson (1979). This book includes excerpts from the 'Threshold Level' (see also chapter 7). Brief reviews of some main aspects of communicative language teaching are given by Johnson (1979) and Littlewood (1978b). There are some short introductory papers in Johnson and Morrow (1978). Brumfit (1978) gives a general assessment of its assumptions and contributions. Canale and Swain (1980) provide a useful overview and discussion of its theoretical bases.

The reader who is interested in a communicative approach to English for specific purposes can turn to Holden (1977), Jupp and Hodlin (1975) and Mackay and Mountford (1978). For a communicative approach to the written word, see White (1980), Widdowson (1978) and some papers in Widdowson (1979). A communicative approach to testing is discussed by Morrow (1979) and Oller (1979). Brown (1980) discusses the principles which underlie language learning.

Chapter 1

Useful discussions of the 'functional' view of language can be found in Coulthard (1977), Criper and Widdowson (1975), Robinson (1972) and Widdowson (1972). The nature of communicative ability is discussed briefly by Johnson (1979) and Littlewood (1978a) and in greater theoretical or technical detail by Candlin (1976), Leeson (1975), Littlewood (1979) and Widdowson (1978).

The example of teacher-pupil misunderstanding is taken from Tough (1973, page 41).

Chapter 2

Ways of making controlled language practice more 'meaningful' are discussed by Byrne (1976), Dakin (1973) and Paulston and Bruder (1976). Kerr (1979) contains picture cue-cards as well as useful suggestions for their use.

Some courses which include activities of the kind discussed in this chapter are Abbs et al. (1975ff), BBC (1974ff), Boardman (1979), Johnson and Morrow (1979), Morrow and Johnson (1979) and Watcyn-Jones (1979).

Chapter 3

The place and function of communicative activity in foreign language learning are discussed by Allwright (1977), Brumfit (1978 and 1979), Krashen (1976), Littlewood (1974 and 1975a), Rivers (1972 and 1978) and Savignon (1972).

Chapter 4

Suggestions for activities which involve overcoming an information gap can be found in Byrne and Rixon (1979), several articles in Holden (1978), in Joiner and Westphal (1978) and Wright et al. (1979). Information exchange is involved in some activities in the courses of Johnson and Morrow (1979), Morrow and Johnson (1979) and in Kerr (1979). Ideas can often be found in the more practically oriented magazines and journals, such as *Modern English Teacher*.

'Find Your Partner' and 'Let's Go Together' are described by Byrne (1978b). 'Jigsaw listening' is discussed by Geddes and Sturtridge (1978), who have used the technique as a basis for their teaching materials *Listening Links* (Geddes and Sturtridge 1979). *Interaction Activities* is listed in the bibliography under Kettering (1975); the activities in this course are also discussed by Paulston and Bruder (1976). *Read and Think* is listed under Munby (1968).

The 'Interaction Packages' of Byrne (1978a) contain sets of materials which can be used for some of the types of activity discussed in this chapter (e.g. 'discovering locations' in section 4.2). Useful ideas and materials for implementing them are to be found in *Concept Seven-Nine* (Unit 3: 'Communication'), which was first devised for developing the communication skills of immigrant children in Great Britain (Wight et al. 1972).

Chapter 5

Using the foreign language to teach other school subjects is discussed in
Widdowson (1978). A useful introductory account of 'immersion classes'
in Canada is Stern (1978). Some British and European experiments are
discussed in Hawkins and Perren (1978).

On the preparation and organisation of discussion sessions, see for
example Byrne (1976) and Ur (1980 and 1981). Examples of materials for
stimulating creative discussion are Byrne and Wright (1975), Maley and
Duff (1975 and 1978a), O'Neill and Scott (1974) and Maley, Duff and
Grellet (1980). Textbooks which include discussion as an integral part
of the course include Boardman (1979) and Hicks et al. (1979). The use
of pupils' school experience as a basis for discussion and role-playing is
advocated and illustrated by Black and Butzkamm (1977 and 1978).

Practical aspects of role-playing in foreign language teaching are discussed in a special issue of *ELT Documents* (British Council 1977), also
by Byrne (1976), K. Jones (1979), the handbook of Menné (1975ff), Paulston and Bruder (1976) and Pickering (1979). Aspects of the underlying
rationale are discussed by Pickering (1979) and also by Littlewood
(1975b). Davison and Gordon (1978) and Taylor and Walford (1978)
provide useful treatments of the use of simulation in education, but not
specifically in foreign language teaching; they contain lists of published
simulations. K. Jones (1980) includes discussion related specifically to
foreign language teaching.

Approaches is listed in the bibliography under Johnson and Morrow
(1979) and *Feelings* under Doff and Jones (1980). Other post-intermediate
or advanced courses which make extensive use of role-playing activities
include Boardman (1979), Hicks et al. (1979), Jones (1977 and 1979),
Morrow and Johnson (1979) and Watcyn-Jones (1979). Watcyn-Jones
(1978) is a book of role-plays with an accompanying book of rolecards.
Alexander (1978) and Abbs et al. (1975ff) are examples of courses which
use role-playing in the early stages of learning.

Detective is one of a series of role-playing activities for EFL, called
Q-Cards (Menné 1975ff). *Pop Festival* is one of six role-playing exercises
in *It's Your Choice* (Lynch 1977). *North Sea Exploration* and *North Sea
Challenge* were devised, respectively, by Walford (1973) and Harvey and
Wheeler (1976). Herbert and Sturtridge (1979) contains materials for
four EFL simulations; it also includes a list of other published simulations useful for EFL. The nine simulations in Jones (1975) were devised
for the development of communication skills in the mother tongue and
are also used successfully for foreign language learning.

Numerous ideas for stimulating creative interaction through drama
techniques, including improvisation, are contained in Maley and Duff
(1978b). Improvisation is also discussed in Byrne (1976).

Chapter 6

The nature of listening comprehension is discussed by Maley (1978),
Maley and Moulding (1981) and White (1978), who also make practical

teaching suggestions. Useful ideas are also contained in Mugglestone (1975).

The characteristics of 'normal speech' are analysed by Brown (1977), Crystal and Davy (1975) and Littlewood (1977a, with examples from French). Geddes and White (1978) suggest 'semi-scripted' speech as a way of producing listening materials which are controlled yet show the features of natural speech.

Communicate is listed in the bibliography under Morrow and Johnson (1979), *Starting Strategies* under Abbs et al. (1975ff) and *Listening Links* under Geddes and Sturtridge (1979). The technique of jigsaw listening is also discussed in Geddes and Sturtridge (1978). *Variations on a Theme* is listed under Maley and Duff (1978a). Listening activities of the kind discussed in this chapter can also be found in Alexander (1978), Hicks et al. (1979), Unit 1 ('Listening with Understanding') of *Concept Seven-Nine* (Wight et al. 1972) and Blundell and Stokes (1981). White (1979) makes extensive use of 'information transfer' for practising reading and writing. O'Neill and Scott (1974) contains listening materials which can be used to stimulate discussion.

Methodological arguments in favour of attaching greater importance to receptive skills are offered by Asher et al. (1974), Littlewood (1978c) and Postovsky (1974).

Chapter 7

The Council of Europe's 'Threshold Level' is listed in the bibliography under Van Ek (1975, also 1980). Sections are reprinted in Brumfit and Johnson (1979). The original version is for adults; a version with amendments for younger learners is Van Ek and Alexander (1977a). Useful introductory discussions are Trim (1977), Van Ek (1977) and the papers collected in Council of Europe (1978). An intermediate specification of communicative objectives, representing a target-level half-way towards the Threshold Level, is called 'Waystage'. It is listed under Van Ek and Alexander (1977b, also 1980).

Munby (1978) proposes a model for defining the communicative needs of learners of English for specific purposes; it contains detailed inventories which can be used as check-lists.

Wilkins (1976) has had a wide influence in the field of communicative syllabus design. Shorter discussions by Wilkins are in two papers reprinted in Brumfit and Johnson (1979) and a paper in Johnson and Morrow (1978). The reconciliation of functional and structural principles in organising courses is discussed by Alexander (1976), Johnson (1978) and Johnson's paper in Johnson and Morrow (1978). Shaw (1977) provides a more general overview of developments in syllabus design. Swan (1981) offers a useful assessment of the role of various elements – both communicative and structural – in designing a syllabus. Cook (1978) summarises various approaches.

In the teaching of foreign languages in Great Britain, a significant development is the increasing influence of a movement towards 'defined syllabuses' based on communicative categories. Discussion and references can be found in Harding and Naylor (1979) and the papers in issue No. 19 of *Modern Languages in Scotland* (1980).

Starting Strategies is listed in the bibliography under Abbs et al. (1975ff). Other courses where the early stages of learning are organised around functional as well as structural categories are Alexander (1978) and BBC (1974ff).

Functions of English is listed in the bibliography under Jones (1977), *Vital English* under Morgan and Percil (1977), *Notions in English* under Jones (1979) and *English Topics* under Cook (1974). Other courses for post-intermediate or advanced learners which organise the material around functions, topics or notions include Boardman (1979), Doff and Jones (1980), Hicks et al. (1979), Johnson and Morrow (1979), Morrow and Johnson (1979) and Watcyn-Jones (1979).

Chapter 8

Ways of defining 'communication' for language-teaching purposes are discussed in Littlewood (1977b), Reisener (1972) and Rivers (1972).

The question of the learner's 'internal syllabus' determining the sequence of learning is discussed by Corder (e.g. 1973, 1975 and 1978). Corder also discusses the implications for our attitudes to errors, on which see also James (1977). Several papers relating to these questions can be found in Richards (1974) and Schumann and Stenson (1974).

The need to reduce the teacher's domination of the classroom is considered by Allwright (1977) and Stevick (1976). Stevick discusses this topic as part of a wider discussion of human relationships and affective factors in the classroom. Schumann (1978) summarises evidence about the influence of a variety of psychological and social factors on the process of foreign language learning.

Psychological and interpersonal factors are emphasised in a number of attempts to produce radically different approaches to foreign language teaching. These include Community Language Learning (Curran 1976, La Forge 1979), the Silent Way (Gattegno 1972 and 1976), Suggestopedia (Bushman and Madsen 1976, O'Connell 1978) and the Total Physical Response Approach (Asher et al. 1974). Discussions of these approaches can be found in Stevick (1976 and 1980). Benseler and Schulz (1980) provide a useful survey, with further references, of these and other current methodological trends.

Bibliography

Abbs, B., A. Ayton and I. Freebairn (1975ff). *Strategies* (Book 1: *Starting Strategies,* 1977; Book 2: *Building Strategies,* 1979; Book 3: *Strategies,* 1975). London: Longman.

Alexander, L. G. (1976). 'Where do we go from here? A reconsideration of some basic assumptions affecting course design.' *English Language Teaching Journal* Vol. 30 No. 2, pp. 89–103.

Alexander, L. G. (1978). *Mainline Beginners.* London: Longman.

Allwright, R. L. (1977). 'Language learning through communication practice.' *ELT Documents* (British Council) 76/3, pp. 2–14. Reprinted in Brumfit and Johnson, 1979.

Asher, J. J., J. A. Kusudo and R. De La Torre (1974). 'Learning a second language through commands: the second field test.' *Modern Language Journal* Vol. 58 Nos. 1–2, pp. 24–32.

Benseler, D. P. and R. A. Schulz (1980). 'Methodological trends in college foreign language instruction.' *Modern Language Journal* Vol. 64 No. 1, pp. 88–96.

BBC (1974ff). *Kontakte* (German Course). London: British Broadcasting Corporation.

Black, C. and W. Butzkamm (1977). *Klassengespräche.* Heidelberg: Quelle & Meyer.

Black, C. and W. Butzkamm (1978). 'Classroom language: materials for communicative language teaching.' *English Language Teaching Journal* Vol. 32 No. 4, pp. 270–274.

Blatchford, C. H. (1976). 'The Silent Way and teacher training.' In J. F. Fanselow and R. H. Crymes (eds.) *On TESOL '76.* Washington: TESOL.

Blundell, L. and J. Stokes (1981). *Task Listening.* Cambridge University Press.

Boardman, R. (1979). *Over to You.* Cambridge University Press.

British Council (1977). 'Games, simulations and role-playing.' Special Issue of *ELT Documents* (77/1).

Brown, G. (1977). *Listening to Spoken English.* London: Longman.

Brown, H. D. (1980). *Principles of Language Learning and Teaching.* New Jersey: Prentice Hall.

Brumfit, C. J. (1978). 'Communicative language teaching: an assessment.' In P. Strevens (ed.) *In Honour of A. S. Hornby.* Oxford University Press.

Brumfit, C. J. (1979). 'Communicative language teaching: an educational perspective.' In Brumfit and Johnson, 1979.

Brumfit, C. J. and K. Johnson (eds.) (1979). *The Communicative Approach to Language Teaching.* Oxford University Press.

Bushman, R. W. and H. S. Madsen (1976). 'A description and evaluation of Suggestopedia — a new teaching methodology.' In J. F. Fanselow and R. H. Crymes (eds.) *On TESOL '76.* Washington: TESOL.

101

Byrne, D. (1976). *Teaching Oral English*. London: Longman.

Byrne, D. (1978a). *Materials for Language Teaching: Interaction Packages*. London: Modern English Publications.

Byrne, D. (1978b). 'Three interaction activities.' In Holden, 1978.

Byrne, D. and S. Rixon (1979). *Communication Games*. Windsor: NFER.

Byrne, D. and A. Wright (1975). *What Do You Think?* London: Longman.

Canale, M. and M. Swain (1980). 'Theoretical bases of communicative approaches to second language teaching and testing.' *Applied Linguistics* Vol. 1 No. 1, pp. 1–47.

Candlin, C. N. (1976). 'Communicative language teaching and the debt to pragmatics.' In C. Rameh (ed.) *Georgetown University Round Table 1976*. Georgetown University Press.

Cook, V. J. (1974). *English Topics*. Oxford University Press.

Cook, V. J. (1978). 'Some ways of organising language.' *Audio-Visual Language Journal* Vol. 16 No. 2, pp. 89–94.

Corder, S. P. (1973). *Introducing Applied Linguistics*. Harmondsworth: Penguin Books.

Corder, S. P. (1975). 'Error analysis, interlanguage and second language acquisition.' *Language Teaching and Linguistics: Abstracts* Vol. 8 No. 4, pp. 201–218.

Corder, S. P. (1978). 'Language-learner language.' In J. C. Richards (ed.) *Understanding Second and Foreign Language Learning*. Rowley, Mass.: Newbury House.

Coulthard, M. (1977). *An Introduction to Discourse Analysis*. London: Longman.

Council of Europe (1978). *A European Unit/Credit System for Modern Language Learning by Adults*. Strasbourg: Council of Europe.

Criper, C. and H. Widdowson (1975). 'Sociolinguistics and language teaching.' In J. P. B. Allen and S. P. Corder (eds.) *Papers in Applied Linguistics*. Oxford University Press.

Crystal, D. and D. Davy (1975). *Advanced Conversational English*. London: Longman.

Curran, C. (1976). *Counselling-Learning in Second Languages*. Apple River, Illinois: Apple River Press.

Dakin, J. (1973). *The Language Laboratory and Language Learning*. London: Longman.

Davison, A. and P. Gordon (1978). *Games and Simulation in Action*. London: Woburn Press.

Doff, A. and C. Jones (1980). *Feelings*. Cambridge University Press.

Gattegno, C. (1972). *Teaching Foreign Languages in Schools: the Silent Way*. New York: Educational Solutions.

Gattegno, C. (1976). *The Common Sense of Teaching Foreign Languages*. New York: Educational Solutions.

Geddes, M. and G. Sturtridge (1978). 'Jigsaw listening and oral communication.' *Modern English Teacher* Vol. 6 No. 1, pp. 4–6.

Geddes, M. and G. Sturtridge (1976). *Listening Links*. London: Heinemann.

Geddes, M. and R. V. White (1978). 'The use of semi-scripted simulated authentic speech and listening comprehension.' *Audio-Visual Language Journal* Vol. 16 No. 3, pp. 137–145.

Harding, A. and J. Naylor (1979). 'Graded objectives in second language teaching.' *Audio-Visual Language Journal* Vol. 17 No. 2, pp. 169–174.

Harvey, G. M. and M. S. Wheeler (1976). *North Sea Challenge* (Language Training Pack). London: B.P. Educational Service.

Hawkins, E. W. and G. E. Perren (eds.) (1978). *Intensive Language Teaching in Schools.* London: CILT.

Herbert, D. and G. Sturtridge (1979). *Simulations.* Windsor: NFER.

Hicks, D., M. Poté, A. Esnol and D. Wright (1979). *A Case for English.* Cambridge University Press.

Holden, S. (ed.) (1977). *English for Specific Purposes.* London: Modern English Publications.

Holden, S. (ed.) (1978). *Visual Aids for Classroom Interaction.* London: Modern English Publications.

James, C. (1977). 'Judgments of error gravities.' *English Language Teaching Journal* Vol. 31 No. 2, pp. 116–124.

Johnson, K. (1978). 'Syllabus design and the adult beginner.' *Modern English Teacher* Vol. 6 No. 2, pp. 19–22.

Johnson, K. (1979). 'Communicative approaches and communicative processes.' In Brumfit and Johnson, 1979.

Johnson, K. and K. Morrow (eds.) (1978). *Functional Materials and the Classroom Teacher.* Centre for Applied Language Studies, University of Reading.

Johnson, K. and K. Morrow (1979). *Approaches.* Cambridge University Press.

Joiner, E. G. and P. B. Westphal (eds.) (1978). *Developing Communication Skills.* Rowley, Mass.: Newbury House.

Jones, K. (1975). *Nine Simulations.* Bedford: Management Games Ltd (formerly published by Inner London Education Authority).

Jones, K. (1979). 'Spotting a good simulation.' *Modern English Teacher* Vol. 7 No. 1, pp. 28–29.

Jones, K. (1980). *Simulations: A Handbook for Teachers.* London: Kogan Page.

Jones, L. (1977, 1981 new edn). *Functions of English.* Cambridge University Press.

Jones, L. (1979). *Notions in English.* Cambridge University Press.

Jupp, T. C. and S. Hodlin (1975). *Industrial English.* London: Heinemann.

Kerr, J. Y. K. (1979). *Picture Cue Cards for Oral Language Practice.* London: Evans Brothers.

Kettering, J. C. (1975). *Developing Communicative Competence: Interaction Activities in English as a Second Language.* Center for International Studies, University of Pittsburgh.

Krashen, S. D. (1976). 'Formal and informal linguistic environments in language acquisition and language learning.' *TESOL Quarterly* Vol. 10 No. 2, pp. 157–168.

La Forge, P. G. (1979). 'Reflection in the context of Community Language Learning.' *English Language Teaching Journal* Vol. 33 No. 4, pp. 247–254.

Leeson, R. (1975). *Fluency and Language Teaching.* London: Longman.

Littlewood, W. T. (1974). 'Communicative competence and grammatical accuracy in foreign language learning.' *Educational Review* Vol. 27 No. 1, pp. 34–44.

Littlewood, W. T. (1975a). 'The acquisition of communicative competence in an artificial environment.' *Praxis* (Dortmund) Vol. 22 No. 1, pp. 13–21.

Littlewood, W. T. (1975b). 'Role performance and language teaching.' *IRAL* Vol. 13 No. 3, pp. 199–208.

Littlewood, W. T. (1977a). 'Some linguistic factors in listening comprehension.' *Audio-Visual Language Journal* Vol. 15 No. 2, pp. 170–174.

Littlewood, W. T. (1977b). 'Defining "communication" in foreign language teaching.' *Linguistische Berichte* No. 52, pp. 83–91.

Littlewood, W. T. (1978a). 'Oral communication ability.' *Modern Languages* Vol. 59 No. 1, pp. 28–33.

Littlewood, W. T. (1978b). 'Communicative language teaching.' *Audio-Visual Language Journal* Vol. 16 No. 3, pp. 131–135.

Littlewood, W. T. (1978c). 'Receptive skills as an objective for slow learners.' *Der fremdsprachliche Unterricht* No. 46, pp. 11–20.

Littlewood, W. T. (1979). 'Communicative performance in language-developmental contexts.' *IRAL* Vol. 17 No. 2, pp. 123–138.

Lynch, M. (1977). *It's Your Choice*. London: Edward Arnold.

Mackay, R. and A. Mountford (eds.) (1978). *English for Specific Purposes*. London: Longman.

Maley, A. (1978). 'The teaching of listening comprehension skills.' *Modern English Teacher* Vol. 6 No. 3, pp. 6–9.

Maley, A. and A. Duff (1975). *Sounds Interesting*. Cambridge University Press.

Maley, A. and A. Duff (1978a). *Variations on a Theme*. Cambridge University Press.

Maley, A. and A. Duff (1978b). *Drama Techniques in Language Learning*. Cambridge University Press.

Maley, A. and A. Duff (1979). *Sounds Intriguing*. Cambridge University Press.

Maley, A., A. Duff and F. Grellet (1980). *The Mind's Eye*. Cambridge University Press.

Maley, A. and S. Moulding (1981) *Learning to Listen*. Cambridge University Press.

Menné, S. (1975ff). *Q-Cards*. Tenterden, Kent: Paul Norbury.

Morgan, M. L. and J. J. Percil (1977). *Vital English*. London: Macmillan.

Morrow, K. (1979). 'Communicative language testing: revolution or evolution?' In Brumfit and Johnson, 1979.

Morrow, K. and K. Johnson (1979). *Communicate*. Cambridge University Press.

Mugglestone, P. (1975). 'Active listening exercises.' *Modern English Teacher* Vol. 3 No. 2, pp. 7–8.

Munby, J. (1968). *Read and Think*. London: Longman.

Munby, J. (1978). *Communicative Syllabus Design*. Cambridge University Press.

O'Connell, P. (1978). 'Bearing gifts from Bulgaria.' *Times Educational Supplement,* 11 August, pp. 27–28.

Oller, J. (1979). *Language Tests at School*. London: Longman.

O'Neill, R. and R. Scott (1974). *Viewpoints*. London: Longman.

Paulston, C. B. and M. N. Bruder (1976). *Teaching English as a Second Language: Techniques and Procedures*. Cambridge, Mass.: Winthrop.

Bibliography

Pickering, M. (1979). 'Role-playing as a technique in foreign language teaching.' *Tempus* (Helsinki) Vol. 14 No. 4, pp. 9–13, and No. 5, pp. 5–8.

Postovsky, V. A. (1974). 'Effects of delay in oral practice at the beginning of second language learning.' *Modern Language Journal* Vol. 58 Nos. 5–6, pp. 229–239.

Reisener, H. (1972). 'Zur Definition von Kommunikation als Lernziel für den Fremdsprachenunterricht.' *Die Neuren Sprachen* No. 4 (Neue Folge), pp. 197–202.

Richards, J. C. (ed.) (1974). *Error Analysis.* London: Longman.

Rivers, W. M. (1972). *Speaking in Many Tongues.* Rowley, Mass.: Newbury House.

Rivers, W. M. (1978). *A Practical Guide to the Teaching of English as a Second or Foreign Language.* Oxford University Press.

Robinson, W. P. (1972). *Language and Social Behaviour.* Harmondsworth: Penguin Books.

Savignon, S. (1972). 'Teaching for communicative competence: a research report.' *Audio-Visual Language Journal* Vol. 10 No. 3, pp. 153–162.

Schumann, J. H. (1978). 'Social and psychological factors in second language acquisition.' In J. C. Richards (ed.) *Understanding Second and Foreign Language Learning.* Rowley, Mass.: Newbury House.

Schumann, J. H. and N. Stenson (eds.) (1974). *New Frontiers in Second Language Learning.* Rowley, Mass.: Newbury House.

Shaw, A. (1977). 'Foreign language syllabus development: some recent approaches'. *Language Teaching and Linguistics: Abstracts* Vol. 10 No. 4, pp. 217–233.

Stern, H. H. (1978). 'French immersion in Canada: achievements and directions.' *Canadian Modern Language Review* Vol. 34 No. 5, pp. 836–854.

Stevick, E. W. (1976). *Memory, Meaning and Method.* Rowley, Mass.: Newbury House.

Stevick, E. W. (1980). *A Way and Ways.* Rowley, Mass.: Newbury House.

Swan, M. (1981). 'Communicative or structural – a false opposition.' In K. Johnson and K. Morrow (eds.) *Communication in the Classroom.* London: Longman.

Taylor, J. L. and R. Walford (1978). *Learning and the Simulation Game.* Milton Keynes: Open University Press. (First published in 1972 by Penguin Books, under the title *Simulation in the Classroom.*)

Tough, J. (1973). *Focus on Meaning.* London: Allen & Unwin.

Trim, J. L. M. (1977). 'A European unit credit system.' *Modern Languages in Scotland* No. 14, pp. 39–44. Also in Council of Europe, 1978.

Ur, P. (1980). 'The conversation class.' *Modern English Teacher* Vol. 7 No. 4, pp. 5–7.

Ur, P. (1981). *Discussions that Work.* Cambridge University Press.

Van Ek, J. (1975). *Systems Development in Adult Language Learning: The Threshold Level.* Strasbourg: Council of Europe. Also published by Pergamon, 1980.

Van Ek, J. (1977). 'The Threshold Level.' *Modern Languages in Scotland* No. 14, pp. 44–50. Also in Council of Europe, 1978.

Van Ek, J. and L. G. Alexander (1977a). *The Threshold Level for Modern Language Teaching in Schools*. London: Longman.

Van Ek, J. and L. G. Alexander (1977b). *Systems Development in Adult Language Learning: Waystage*. Strasbourg: Council of Europe. Also published by Pergamon, 1980.

Walford, R. (1973). *North Sea Exploration* (Longman Simulation Pack 2). London: Longman.

Watcyn-Jones, P. (1978). *Act English*. Harmondsworth: Penguin Books.

Watcyn-Jones, P. (1979). *Impact*. Harmondsworth: Penguin Books.

White, R. V. (1978). 'Listening comprehension and note-taking.' *Modern English Teacher* Vol. 6 No. 1, pp. 23–27, and No. 2, pp. 22–24.

White, R. V. (1979). *Functional English* (Books 1 and 2). Sunbury on Thames: Nelson.

White, R. V. (1980). *Teaching Written English*. London: Allen & Unwin.

Widdowson, H. G. (1972). 'The teaching of English as communication.' *English Language Teaching* Vol. 27 No. 1, pp. 15–19. Reprinted in Brumfit and Johnson, 1979.

Widdowson, H. G. (1978). *Teaching Language as Communication*. Oxford University Press.

Widdowson, H. G. (1979). *Explorations in Applied Linguistics*. Oxford University Press.

Wight, J., R. A. Norris and F. J. Worsley (1972). *Concept Seven-Nine*. Leeds: E. J. Arnold and Schools Council.

Wilkins, D. A. (1976). *Notional Syllabuses*. Oxford University Press.

Wright, A., D. Betteridge and M. Buckby (1979). *Games for Language Learning*. Cambridge University Press.

Index